Crusade 2.0

Crusade 2.0

The West's Resurgent War against Islam

John Feffer

City Lights Books | Open Media Series

The Open Media Series is edited by Greg Ruggiero and archived by the Tamiment Library, New York University.

Cover design by Pollen

Library of Congress Cataloging-in-Publication Data
Feffer, John.
 Crusade 2.0 : the West's unending war against Islam / John Feffer.
     p. cm. — (Open media series)
 ISBN 978-0-87286-545-7
1. Islamic countries—Foreign relations—United States. 2. United
States—Foreign relations—Islamic countries. 3. Islam—Foreign
public opinion. I. Title.

 DS35.74.U6F44 2012
 303.48'2182101767—dc23

                          2011045458

City Lights Books are published at the City Lights Bookstore
261 Columbus Avenue, San Francisco, CA 94133
www.citylights.com

*For Edith Feffer, who taught me
to challenge injustice*

Contents

Introduction
Target: Islam

It was the Summer of Hate, and the target was Islam.

The television news coverage in the United States during the summer of 2010 was full of images of angry Americans waving signs that denounced the world's second largest religion. The fury seemed to come out of nowhere. Unfavorable attitudes toward Islam had been steadily dropping among people in the U.S.[1] In 2009, looking back at a two-year decline in hate crimes against Muslims, a prominent monitoring organization expressed "its cautious optimism that America may be witnessing a leveling-off of the post-9/11 backlash against Americans of the Islamic faith."[2]

The optimism was premature.

In June 2010, picketers began to protest the construction of Park51, a Muslim community center in lower Manhattan, and the media was aflame with the controversy. By the end of August, in Murfreesboro, Tennessee, very real flames licked at the construction site of another Islamic center, courtesy of unknown vandals. It was only the latest in a series of attacks that included an attempted firebombing of an Islamic center in Florida in May and vandalism against mosques in Wisconsin, Michigan, and Texas.[3] Also over the summer, Florida pastor Terry Jones and his tiny fundamentalist flock decided to play with fire by vowing to burn copies of the Qur'an on the anniversary of 9/11. Concerned that this act of desecration would provoke attacks against U.S. soldiers in Afghanistan and Iraq, President Barack Obama put pressure on the pastor to cancel the event.

The fearmongers employed other tactics that summer. Protesters brought in dogs because "Muslims hate dogs"—to demonstrate their opposition to a new mosque in Temecula, California.[4] A group called Stop Islamization of America bought anti-Islamic ads on busses in San Francisco, Miami, and New York.[5] Even in Oklahoma, where less than 1 percent of the population is Muslim, a movement coalesced around an improbable referendum to ban *sharia* (Islamic law) that passed decisively in the November mid-term elections.[6]

Meanwhile, public personalities were engaged in an informal competition to see who could make the most offensive comments about Islam. Presidential hopeful Newt Gingrich compared the organizers of the Park51 center to Nazis. Talk show host Rush Limbaugh called the interfaith center a "victory monument at Ground Zero." Evangelist Franklin Graham repeatedly referred to Islam as an "evil" religion.[7] When President Obama proclaimed at an *iftar* ceremony breaking the Ramadan fast that "Muslims have the same right to practice their religion as everyone else in this country," former cold warrior Frank Gaffney responded that this remark proved that the president "sided with *shariah*."[8] Indeed, the anti-Islamic sentiment bubbling up in the United States in 2010 was beginning to rival the anti-communist hysteria of the Cold War era, with figures like Gaffney indulging in the religious equivalent of red-baiting.

And it was having an impact on public opinion. The decline in unfavorable attitudes toward Islam made a sharp reversal that year.[9] On August 19, 2010, *Time* devoted an article to whether "America has a Muslim problem." By the end of the month, Islamophobia had graduated to the cover of the magazine.[10]

The situation was even uglier in Europe. Legislatures in Belgium, France, and Spain debated bills on restricting Muslim dress, which came on the heels of a move by Switzerland to ban minaret construction. Right-wing parties espousing anti-immigrant and anti-Islamic views were attracting wider followings. European publics simultaneously wanted to withdraw their troops from the allied war effort in Afghanistan and limit further European integration by keeping Turkey out of the European Union, and populists were exploiting these views to promote their own vision of Fortress Europe.

Islamophobia didn't go away after 2010's Summer of Hate. True, Park51 eventually opened a year later without any major incidents. But in other respects, the fury didn't subside. Terry Jones followed through on his pledge, burning a Qur'an in March 2011 and generating a worldwide backlash that killed more than a dozen people.[11] Nearly two dozen states copied Oklahoma's example by introducing anti-*sharia* legislation. Congress picked up on the theme, with Rep. Peter King (R-NY) holding controversial hearings in March 2011 on the "radicalization" of American Muslims. Several Republican presidential candidates indulged in anti-Islamic sentiment, with Herman Cain going so far as to pledge not to appoint Muslims to office (a position he later recanted). Right-wing foundations were pouring more than $40 million into anti-Islamic efforts.[12] And in Europe, anti-Islamic bestsellers, violent street protests, and even a mass killing in Norway all kept the fires of Islamophobia burning.

For some, the explanation for these anti-Islamic outbursts is simple. Americans and Europeans are still angry about 9/11 and the subsequent terrorist bombings in London and Madrid. They are still outraged over the 2004 murder of Dutch filmmaker Theo van Gogh by Mohammed Bouyeri, a Dutch-Moroccan Muslim. They are fearful of al-Qaeda and the Taliban, Iranian leader Mahmoud Ahmadinejad, the Gaza-based Hamas and the Beirut-based Hezbollah. They are concerned about the individuals who have instigated or planned recent attacks, including a shooting at Fort Hood in Texas, suicide bombings in Moscow and Stockholm, an attempt to explode a bomb in New York's Times Square, and schemes to blow up the Washington DC metro and a Christmas ceremony in Portland, Oregon. The problem, for those who try to rationalize the anger in this way, lies with Muslims and their so-called penchant for violence.

Another simple explanation for the surge of Islamophobia in 2010 and after is the rise of the Tea Party movement and its polarization of the electorate. The severe economic downturn following the financial crisis of 2008 allowed for the populism of resentment to flourish. The election of a president that nearly one-quarter of the U.S. electorate still falsely believed in August 2010 was Muslim provided a political opportunity for anti–Democratic Party activists to play the religion card.[13] These same activists have intensified their efforts to discredit the president and his party in the run-up to the 2012 presidential elections.

The mistaken belief that al-Qaeda and the Fort Hood shooter represent Islam and its more than 1.5 billion adherents worldwide has certainly played a role in maintaining high levels of fear and animosity in the United States and Europe.[14] The anti-Islamic statements of politicians and the politically motivated organizing of far-right-wing activists have also strongly influenced media coverage and public opinion.

But anti-Islamic sentiment runs much deeper in Western culture and society. Rather than inhabiting only the lunatic fringe, Islamophobia is sustained by U.S. government policy, particularly its wars and counterterrorism efforts, and by analysts firmly in the mainstream. And it draws on myths and misconceptions that go back a thousand years and more. The hate that spiked in the summer of 2010 didn't come from nowhere.

The Geopolitical Context

The Middle East is embroiled in conflict. Islam is on the rise, yet again, and a new Islamic movement has emerged in central Anatolia that challenges the established order. The West, divided by several different factions, is expending considerable resources on war in the region. Prominent Western voices warn of a Muslim take-over of Europe, of a violent attempt to create a global caliphate. Those of a more apocalyptic bent argue that the fate of Western civilization itself hangs in the balance.

Welcome to the twenty-first century? Actually, try the eleventh.

In 1095, in response to the Seljuk Turks seizing Jerusalem and other cities, Christendom launched its first Crusade against the Islamic world. More than half a dozen military campaigns followed over the next several hundred years in a conflict that defined not only the Middle Ages but the very contours of Western identity. This era of Crusade 1.0 lasted almost a thousand years until the fall of the Ottoman Empire and Turkey's subsequent abolition of the Islamic caliphate in 1924.

The wheel of history has circled around. Islam is again resurgent and again in the crosshairs of the West. We are now enmeshed in a second major confrontation, Crusade 2.0. The war in Afghanistan has already become America's longest military conflict. The other "overseas contingency operations" launched by the United States and its allies, which have replaced the "global war on terror," promise to last even longer and determine the shape of what has been called the post-post–Cold War era.

Today, as in the eleventh century, the West imagines that it's involved in a war without end and without borders, a war of good against evil, a war that defines the very essence of civilization.

Although similar in important respects to the medieval holy war, Crusade 2.0 is not simply the Tenth Crusade.[15] In 1095, there were no large populations of Muslims living in the West under Christian dominion, and the West did not shrink from declaring Islam the enemy. Today, by contrast, the U.S. government and its allies in Western Europe and elsewhere try not to mention the "c" word, at least in part because so many Muslims now live in the West. Alliance leaders instead insist that they are fighting terrorism, not Islam, and are committed to winning Muslim "hearts and minds" through military stabilization, economic development, democracy promotion, and public relations campaigns. Despite these efforts, however, many Muslims feel as though they are the victims of a coordinated campaign of air strikes from above and Islamophobic slurs from below.

For optimists, the U.S. election results of 2008 were supposed to bring this two-pronged campaign to an end. Newly elected President Barack Obama promised to draw down the war in Iraq. He pledged to close the Guantánamo detention facility and end torture. Within a few months in office, the Obama administration quietly retired the phrase "global war on terror," and the president spoke in Cairo of reaching out in new ways to the Muslim world. Before it had even reached the ten-year mark, Crusade 2.0 looked to be heading for early retirement.

But the crusade marches on. The Obama administration has continued the wars started by its predecessor un-

der the new name of "overseas contingency operations."
Today, the United States and allies are still fighting wars in
the predominantly Muslim countries of Afghanistan, Pakistan, and Iraq. Under Obama, Special Forces operations
have expanded to a broader swath of the Muslim world
from North Africa to the Far East. His administration has
launched eight times more CIA-directed drone attacks in
Pakistan than its predecessor did over two terms.[16] The
targeted assassination program, which has killed Osama
bin Laden and other top al-Qaeda leaders, has resulted
in civilian casualties, popular outrage, and legal concerns.
Although the administration has made much of a public
diplomacy initiative to engage the Muslim world, U.S. favorability rating in most majority Muslim countries has
only fallen further from its dismal levels during the Bush
years. In Egypt, for instance, U.S. favorability fell from
30 percent in 2006 to 17 percent in 2010 and in Pakistan
from 27 percent to 17 percent over the same period.[17] Even
U.S. support for the uprisings against authoritarian leaders in the Middle East in 2011—the Arab Spring that began in Tunisia and spread to Egypt, Yemen, Syria, Libya,
and elsewhere—has not fundamentally changed attitudes
in the Muslim world. The United States only belatedly
backed these democracy movements, and continued support for authoritarian leaders in Bahrain, Saudi Arabia,
and elsewhere has underscored the U.S. double standard
on democracy in the region.

Within the United States, meanwhile, a vocal minority has successfully imposed its crusader mentality on a

credulous population. Some of the anti-Islamic sentiment has been partisan. According to an August 2010 *Newsweek* poll, a majority of Republicans believed that the president "definitely" or "probably" sympathized with Islamic fundamentalists and their goal to spread *sharia* law across the globe.[18] But it's not just Republicans. Two-thirds of the country confesses to being prejudiced about Muslims.[19]

This book is an attempt to understand the sources of this anti-Islamic sentiment. It will explore the enduring influence of the three unfinished wars of the last millennium—the Crusades, the Cold War, and the war on terrorism—on what we do and how we think in the West. These experiences have produced different types of Islamophobia in Europe and the United States. But the demographic anxiety of the former and the declining relative power of the latter have intersected to amplify the fear of Islam.

In the pages to follow, I argue that the new Crusaders are not primarily concerned about "Islamofascism" or however else they characterize the radical elements of Islam they dislike. The campaign that exploded in the headlines in summer 2010 and has continued to burn through society today has not been about terrorism. It has not been about Islamic extremists attempting to reestablish the caliphate or impose Islamic law on the unwilling. What really keeps Islamophobes up at night is the growing economic, political, and global influence of modern, mainstream Islam.

Consider the recent targets of anti-Islamic sentiment. Right-wing groups—and ultimately more mainstream organizations such as the Anti-Defamation League—singled out a proposed Islamic center in lower Manhattan that is the brainchild of a proponent of interfaith dialogue. This, not a hotbed of radical Islam, stimulated their wrath. The Florida preacher and his followers announced their intention to burn not a book of Osama bin Laden's writings but the Qur'an itself. Liberal intellectual Paul Berman has devoted thousands of words to challenging the reputation of one of the foremost mainstream Muslim theologians, Tariq Ramadan, rather than one of the ideologists of al-Qaeda.

And the country that has caused the greatest fear and trembling in European capitals is not Saudi Arabia or Yemen. Rather, it is Turkey. Although it has moved decisively *away* from authoritarianism and *toward* liberal democracy under the leadership of an Islam-influenced political party, Turkey has become the *bête noire* of Islamophobes intent on "saving" Western civilization.

A New Crusade?

Crusade 1.0 was not a simple "clash of civilizations" between cross and crescent. Although religion certainly played a motivating factor, the Crusades were also about the more mundane objectives associated with war: power, territory, economic gain. These grubbier motives prompted Crusaders sometimes to attack other Christians and sometimes even to ally with Muslims for tactical reasons. But the *image* of the Crusade that comes down to us today is that of a concerted effort to save civilization from the infidel.

Our current crusade—Crusade 2.0—is similarly complicated. The United States has gone to war in defense of a different professed faith, not Christianity but rather liberal democracy. But this professed faith also conceals less noble designs. Like the original Crusaders, the United States and its European partners have been concerned with geopolitical advantage in a strategically important area of the world. For the Crusaders, Jerusalem and its environs were an important pilgrimage site but also a vital trade route. Today's Crusaders have been more concerned about energy sources, whether the oil of Iraq or the natural gas pipelines that pass through Central Asia. To realize these more mundane goals, the West has made certain tactical alliances with actors in the Muslim world—the Northern Alliance in Afghanistan, Sunni fighters in Iraq, and the illiberal governments of Saudi Arabia, Bahrain, and Yemen. These Pentagon counterinsurgency efforts to partner with Muslim governments and Muslims on the ground often put the U.S. military at cross-purposes with Islamophobes. As *New York Times* columnist Frank Rich puts it, "How do you win Muslim hearts and minds in Kandahar when you are calling Muslims every filthy name in the book in New York?"[20]

But few soldiers enlisted to fight in Afghanistan or Iraq to win Muslim hearts and minds or even to preserve Western access to oil and gas. To justify a war and to mobilize young people to fight, Western governments needed a flesh-and-blood enemy. Citizens would only tolerate a more paranoid national security state at home if it was arrayed against a major enemy in the neighborhood. The grander the war and the more intrusive the national security state, the more epic the enemy needed to be. Osama bin

Laden was not big enough. But bin Laden plus the Taliban plus Saddam Hussein plus Iran and Syria and Hamas and Hezbollah and radical imams in London, New York, and Hamburg raised the stakes considerably. To more closely approximate the world-historical enemies of the twentieth century—fascism and communism—the enemy had to pose a threat not just to territory but to civilization itself.

Like its medieval precursor, then, Crusade 2.0 has its paradoxes and complexities. But the *image* of Crusade 2.0—that of a liberal West battling unreasoning religious fanatics—has proven to be as enduring an ideological frame as the original "clash of civilizations" of the eleventh century.

The current conflicts between the United States and its allies on the one hand and so-called radical Islam on the other are not an inevitable outgrowth of earlier history. After all, with the decline of the Ottoman Empire, the larger narrative of Islam versus the West largely disappeared in the nineteenth century. During the Cold War, as this book will explore in more detail, the United States and Israel actually sided with radical Islam against Arab nationalism. Perhaps more importantly, the religion of the parties arrayed against the United States is incidental, not essential. "The Iraqis have negative attitudes toward the United States because we are occupying their freaking land," Iraqi-born blogger Raed Jarrar told me, "not because they are majority Muslim and we are majority Christian."[21]

In other words, we are experiencing a clash of civilizations not on the ground but only in the violent jihadist visions of warriors in the wild East and wild West. Islamo-phobes and the al-Qaeda leadership, like gunslingers in a terrorized town, share an apocalyptic vision and a prefer-ence for illegal violence that keeps Crusade 2.0 alive. "No negotiations, no conferences and no dialogues"—this slo-gan of Abdullah al-Azzam, Osama bin Laden's mentor, could apply equally to both sides.[22]

What is Islamophobia?

With their irrational fear of spiders, arachnophobes are scared of both harmless daddy longlegs and poisonous brown recluse spiders. In extreme cases, an arachnophobe can break out in a sweat while merely looking at photos of spiders. It is, of course, reasonable to steer clear of poison-ous varieties like black widows. What makes a legitimate fear into an irrational phobia, however, is the tendency to lump all members of a group, spiders or humans, into one lethal category and then to exaggerate how threatening they are. Spider bites, after all, are responsible for at most a handful of fatalities a year in the United States.

Islamophobia, a term coined by a French Orientalist Etienne Dinet in 1922 and made popular by the London-based Runnymede Trust in a 1997 report, is similarly an irrational fear of Islam.[23] Yes, certain Muslim fundamen-talists have carried out terrorist attacks, certain extremists inspired by visions of a "global caliphate" continue to plot new attacks on their perceived enemies, and certain groups like Afghanistan's Taliban practice violently intolerant ver-sions of the religion. But Islamophobes confuse these small parts with the whole and then see terrorist *jihad* under every Islamic pillow. They break out in a sweat at the mere picture of a minaret or *imam*.

"Islamophobia" is an imprecise term. Most arachnophobes avoid spiders, they don't declare war on them. What we see today in the media, at right-wing demonstrations outside of mosques, and in European legislation goes beyond fear of Islam and extends into anger and even hatred. Run-of-the-mill Islamophobes may well simply want to steer clear of Muslims. The organizers of the campaigns have a different, more Crusader-like agenda.

Some try to qualify their Islamophobia. "What I am is an Islamismophobe, or better say an anti-Islamist," writes novelist Martin Amis, "because a phobia is an irrational fear, and it is not irrational to fear something that says it wants to kill you."[24] But as this book will argue, much of the sentiment directed specifically at "Islamism" is ultimately meant for Islam as a whole. In an interview, Amis acknowledged that his animus is not just toward extremists. "The Muslim community will have to suffer until it gets its house in order," he said in 2006. "Not letting them travel. Deportation further down the road. Curtailing of freedoms. Strip-searching people who look like they're from the Middle East or Pakistan."[25] Amis seems to have forgotten the fact that the Muslim community has vigorously and repeatedly denounced terrorism. Meanwhile, blaming an entire community for the actions of a miniscule minority is unconscionable. Imagine the outcry if Amis made the same statement about the Irish after an IRA bombing.

Other writers do not even try to disguise the real target of their attacks. In her book *A God Who Hates*, Syria-born psychiatrist Wafa Sultan writes of the "evils of Islam," which is not a religion but a "political doctrine that imposes itself by force."[26] In *The Trouble with Islam*, journalist Irshad Manji, echoing the Cold War with her description of herself as a "Muslim refusenik," criticizes the "desert mindset" of Islam.[27] Nonie Darwish, an Egyptian-American convert to Christianity, calls Islam "an attack on civilization itself by haters of civilization" in *Now They Call Me Infidel*.[28] These are not screeds published on blogs. All three books have mainstream publishers, and their authors have appeared widely in the media. Using these Muslims and ex-Muslims as their spokespeople, a well-funded network of activists, journalists, and think-tankers has turned Islamophobia into a cottage industry and a budding trans-Atlantic endeavor.

This anti-Islamic sentiment that challenges the very center of Islam, not just its radical fringes, is an outgrowth of a profound cultural anxiety in the West. Our major geopolitical foe, the Soviet Union, disintegrated in the 1990s; our chief geo-economic competitor, China, is also the leading holder of U.S. debt. What's left to serve as an enemy, then, is a new geo-cultural threat that challenges our "way of life." As Columbia University professor Mahmood Mamdani explains, "It is no longer the market (capitalism), nor the state (democracy), but culture (modernity) that is said to be the dividing line between those in favor of a peaceful, civic existence and those inclined to terror."[29]

In other words, according to the Islamophobic worldview, while al-Qaeda poses a military threat and the Muslim Brotherhood a political threat, Islam as a whole threatens the West with a fundamentally cultural threat.

And it isn't simply "their" culture that is at fault. Islamophobes have also taken aim at "multiculturalism," which they believe has allowed radical Islam to slip in through the back door of "moral relativism" to gnaw away at Western civilization from within. Muslim extremists are a rare commodity in the West, so Islamophobes expend as much or more of their venom on the "liberal apologists" who wittingly or not open that back door to the adversary.[30] In the most extreme case in July 2011, right-wing fanatic Anders Behring Breivik took aim not at Norway's Muslim immigrants against which he had fulminated at length but the country's Labor Party for encouraging multiculturalism and immigration. Just as the actions of al-Qaeda and Hamas and Iran's Mahmoud Ahmadinejad are part of a struggle within Islam, Islamophobia is part of a culture war between right and left in the West.

Why This Book?

This book is not designed to introduce readers to Islam or argue for its merits as a religion.[31] Personally I am not religious. Religious movements and figures have indeed generated many admirable causes—Gandhi and the independence struggle in India, Martin Luther King and the civil rights effort, Abdul Ghaffar Khan and his nonviolent movement among Pashtuns.[32] But religious movements and figures have also produced violent, uncompromising ideological wars. All religious beliefs seem to produce extremists, and all religions have at one point or another gone to extremes. Islam is not inherently, eternally, or uniquely violent, any more than the "Judeo-Christian" tradition that sometimes has insisted it to be so. And Islam the religion is only one small part of what takes place in the Muslim world, as Edward Said reminds us, for this world "includes dozens of countries, societies, traditions, languages, and, of course, an infinite number of different experiences."[33]

In the end, attacks on Islam are as much of a challenge to civilization—human civilization—as the threat of extremists carrying the banner of Islam. This challenge embraces all of us, Muslims and non-Muslims, believers and non-believers. Non-Muslims ask Muslims to individually and collectively denounce 9/11 and other terrorist acts. Many Muslims have done so, repeatedly.[34] Non-Muslims must similarly step up to denounce Islamophobia.[35]

Al-Qaeda is real, of course, and so is its desire to inflict harm—not only on the West but on anybody who doesn't agree with its extreme ideology, which includes most of the world's Muslims. By denouncing Islamophobia, we stand with the vast majority of the Muslim world against the intolerance of al-Qaeda, its anti-Semitism and its imperial aspirations. Both al-Qaeda and Islamophobes embrace reactive ideologies that are ultimately on the decline. These belief systems burn bright even as they burn out. But they can both cause great damage as they exit history.

This book tells a different story about the relationship

between Islam and the rest of the world. It focuses on the United States and Europe where Crusade 2.0 rages most fiercely (though a similar book could trace these themes in South Asia, Africa, and the Far East). It is not just a description, however. It is an argument for a new way of engagement animated by genuine respect rather than pallid tolerance. War, division, and isolation are the tactics of Crusade 2.0. We can't effectively counter the ideology of al-Qaeda by adopting the tactics of al-Qaeda. Nor will a "separate but equal" ethos suffice. We need to engage Islam in a post-Crusade, post–Cold War, and post-war-on-terror manner.

We are at a critical juncture. After the polarizing policies of the first decade of the twenty-first century, the United States and Europe can fundamentally redefine their relationship with the Muslim world. This will require not only ending the "war on terror" and not just nipping a new cold war against Islam in the bud. It will require an end to the thousand-year hold that the Crusades have had on the Western imagination.

We are at the very beginning of Crusade 2.0, and it has already had a devastating impact in lives lost and historic opportunities squandered. But we are not doomed to repeat history. We can stop the policies of occupation that have produced such a powerful backlash. We can stop asserting a mythic "Judeo-Christian" tradition that deliberately excludes Islam. And we can stop the artificial division of "us" and "them" by bringing Turkey into the European Union and reaffirming that Europe is a home to Muslims as well.

Islamophobia is not an eternal prejudice that has somehow become a fixed part of the social genome of humanity. The sentiment has waxed and waned over time depending on very particular political projects. By shifting our current political trajectory in the three ways I discuss in this book's conclusion, we can bring Crusade 2.0 to a close. And we can ensure that no further crusades will follow.

ONE

The Myths of Crusade 1.0

The Muslims were bloodthirsty and treacherous. They conducted a sneak attack against Charlemagne's army and slaughtered every single soldier, 20,000 in all. More than a thousand years ago, in the mountain passes of medieval Spain, the Muslim horde cut down the finest soldiers in the Holy Roman Emperor's command, including his brave nephew Roland. Then, according to the famous poem that immortalized the tragedy, Charlemagne exacted his revenge by routing the entire Muslim army.

The *Song of Roland*, an eleventh-century rendering in verse of an eighth-century battle, is a staple of Western Civilization classes at colleges around the country. A "masterpiece of epic drama," in the words of its renowned translator Dorothy Sayers, it provides a handy preface for students before they delve into readings on the Crusades.[1] But the poem has also schooled generations of Judeo-Christians to view Muslims as perfidious enemies who once threatened the very foundations of Western civilization.

The problem is that the whole epic is built on a curious falsehood. The army that fell upon Roland and his

Frankish soldiers was not Muslim at all. In the real battle of 778, the slayers of the Franks were Christian Basques furious at Charlemagne for pillaging their city of Pamplona. Not epic at all, the battle emerged from a parochial dispute in the complex wars of medieval Spain.[2] The Franks were indeed battling Muslim armies in Iberia, but it wasn't a holy war and Charlemagne maintained rather good relations with his counterpart in Baghdad.[3] The *Song of Roland* excised the Basque soldiers from history and conflated the complex politics into something far simpler.[4] Later in the eleventh century, as kings and popes and knights and peasants all prepared to do battle in the First Crusade, an anonymous bard did a final repurposing of the text to serve the needs of an emerging cross-against-crescent holy war.

Today, the Crusades are often portrayed as the archetypal "clash of civilizations" between the followers of Jesus and the followers of Mohammed. In the popular imagination, a Muslim horde bent on swallowing Jerusalem and its environs as an appetizer before proceeding to the European entrée has replaced the very diverse adversaries of the Crusaders. These adversaries included Jews killed in pogroms on the way to Jerusalem, rival Catholics slaughtered in the Balkans and in Constantinople, and Christian heretics hunted down in southern France. In medieval Palestine, the Crusaders also fought against both the Christians and the Jews of the region who often took the side of their Muslim compatriots. Just as Charlemagne's attempt to capture the Moorish Iberian provinces of al-Andalus was more than a simple contest between Christians on one side and Muslims on the other, the Crusades were a truly Byzantine contest of shifting political and religious alliances.

Throughout history, warring parties have turned complicated and often contradictory conflicts into Manichean struggles—to motivate soldiers, open the purse strings of financial backers, and ennoble the otherwise bloodthirsty. No medieval poet was going to feel a stirring in the blood to versify an attack by the Basques. No Crusader was going to sell his property to buy armor and a horse simply to conduct a pogrom against Jews in the nearby village. And the U.S. Congress was not going to authorize an attack against Saddam Hussein in 2003 simply because he was a nasty piece of work. In all three cases, the threat posed by a presumably predatory Islam in al-Andalus, in Jerusalem, and in Baghdad's imagined alliance with al-Qaeda kicked the conflict up several notches.

Similar mythmaking has continued into the Obama era with the transformation of Islam into a violent caricature of itself. We seem to be fixed in a perpetual eleventh-century battle of "us" against "them." Indeed, we still seem to be fighting the three great wars of the millennium, even though two of these conflicts have long been over and the third has been rhetorically reduced to "overseas contingency operations." The Crusades, which finally petered out in the fourteenth century, continue to shape our global imagination today. The Cold War ended in 1991, but key elements of the anticommunism credo have been awkwardly grafted onto the new Islamist adversary. And the global war on terror, which President Obama quietly renamed shortly after taking office, has in fact metastasized into the wars that his administration continues to prosecute in Afghanistan, Pakistan, Yemen, and elsewhere.

As long as our unfinished wars still burn in the collective consciousness—and still rage in Kabul, Sana'a, and the Tribal Areas of Pakistan—Islamophobia will make its impact felt in our media, politics, and daily life. The first set of Crusades pitted a frankly barbaric set of Europeans against a more advanced Islamic civilization and prevented a much more peaceable interrelationship from developing. Crusade 2.0 threatens to create an equally dangerous rift that will continue to consume many lives, waste much wealth, and distort our very understanding of our Western selves.

The Enduring Myths of the Crusades

Phobias have deep roots. The fear that arachnophobes have of spiders often stems from events in a dimly remembered childhood, such as a spider crawling into a crib or dangling above a bowl of curds and whey. Our irrational fear of Islam similarly seems to derive from events that happened in the early days of Western civilization. Several enduring myths inherited from the era of the Crusades constitute the core of Islamophobia today: Muslims are inherently violent, Muslims want to take over the world, and Muslims can't be trusted. These myths have been nurtured by some of the most prominent figures in the Western tradition. Marco Polo, who had praise for virtually everything he saw on his thirteenth-century travels eastward including the ruthless Kublai Khan, reserved harsh words only for "the accursed sect of the Saracens, which indulge them in the commission of every crime, and allow them to murder those who differ from them on points of faith."[5] Voltaire, a leading figure of the Enlightenment, wrote a five-act play in 1736 entitled *Fanaticism, or Mahomet the Prophet*. Even the sober German sociologist Max Weber considered Islam a "warrior religion."[6] These are deeply entrenched myths, indeed.

It doesn't take a psychologist to realize that the characteristics ascribed to the devilish Muslim are precisely the ones that the finger-pointers, at some subconscious level, suspect apply to their sainted selves. After all, the violence of the Crusaders was legendary. Nor were the pope and his legions shy about their desire to spread Christendom to every corner of the globe. And the tendency of Crusaders to go back on their word created a deep impression on the Muslim world. The same mirror phenomenon applies today as well. Our modern-day Crusaders deploy extraordinary violence in the wars in Afghanistan and Iraq, have promoted global campaigns on behalf of democracy, liberalism, or Christianity, and have lied to the public, for instance, about Saddam Hussein's nuclear program and his connections to al-Qaeda.

Analyzing these Crusader myths is not only an exercise in historical truth-telling. It is a crucial step in weaning the West off its current delusions. As all recovery programs insist, moving on can't happen without an acknowledgment of addiction. And we've been dangerously addicted to these myths about Islam and Muslims.

Let's begin with the myth of the inherent violence of Islam. The depiction of Islam as a "religion of the sword" was a staple of medieval literature and art.[7] According to one particularly gory version of Pope Urban II's exhortation in 1095 for his followers to embark on the First Crusade, the defilers of the Holy Land were guilty of unspeakable horrors: "When they wish to torture people by a base death, they perforate their navels, and dragging forth the extremity of the intestines, bind it to a stake; then with flogging they lead the victim around until the viscera having gushed forth the victim falls prostrate upon the ground."[8] Not much had changed by the end of the Crusades, though the language was somewhat more circumspect. In the fourteenth century, the Byzantine emperor Manuel II said: "Show me just what Muhammad brought that was new, and there you will find things only evil and inhuman, such as his command to spread by the sword the faith he preached."[9]

It was popular in the Middle Ages—as it is popular today—to identify the Qur'an as the inspiration for these violent tendencies. In one oft-quoted passage, for instance, the Qur'an calls on believers to "slay the idolaters wherever you find them. Arrest them, besiege them, and lie in ambush everywhere for them."[10] Of course, "idolaters" in this infamous "sword verse" means polytheists, the primary enemy of Mohammed and his followers in seventh-century Arabia, not "people of the Book" as Christians and Jews were known.[11] Less frequently cited is the rest of the passage, which recommends coexistence with those who repent and pray according to their tradition and emphasizes the importance of abiding by treaties ("so long as they keep faith with you, keep faith with them").[12]

The "sword verse" does urge violence. But it is balanced by other verses that clearly identify Islam as a religion of peace that forbids the killing of innocent people.[13] According to historian Ayesha Jala, prohibitions *against* warring occur far more often in the Qur'an than exhortations to armed struggle; as Islamic law specialist Khaled Abou El Fadl further notes, every reference to war in the text "is qualified by some moral condition of restraint."[14] These mixed messages might also reflect different philosophies held by different groups of believers at the time.[15]

The Qur'an is not very different from other religious texts. Jewish scripture contains passages that, like the Qur'an, are of surpassing poetry. But it also contains passages of not only violence but, frankly, genocide. Yahweh, for instance, commands Saul to put the Amalekites under a "ban"—to kill all men, women, children, and livestock—and then grows furious when Saul saves the Amalekite king and a few animals.[16] The Jewish kingdom of Israel, like the Islamic caliphate, expanded and consolidated its power through such wars of conquest. But aside from those who harbor anti-Jewish views, it's rare to hear talk of Judaism as a religion of the sword or the conflation of the acts of a few (terrorist Baruch Goldstein, for example, who killed twenty-nine Muslims in the 1994 Hebron massacre) with the religion of an entire people.

If both the Qur'an and Jewish scripture have their

grislier passages, what then of Christians' New Testament? Generally, the message of Jesus in the Bible is one of peace, of turning the other cheek. However, in the last book of the New Testament, the tone shifts considerably. According to the Book of Revelations, in the "first battle of the End," a white horse bearing a mighty warrior issues forth from heaven and from his mouth comes "a sharp sword to strike the pagans with."[17] Unlike the historical description of Saul's exploits in Jewish scripture, this passage cannot be dismissed as belonging to the violence of the time. The Book of Revelations describes the inevitable violence that will drown a future world in blood, an apocalyptic tradition that has inspired much bloodletting.

The First Crusade, for instance, took place at a time of plagues and portents that reinforced the medieval belief that, a thousand years after the death of Jesus, the end was nigh and a campaign against the Antichrist could help bring the sinful world to its climax.[18] Apocalyptic bloodletting came early on in the First Crusade. After just managing to wrest the city of Antioch back from its Muslim rulers in 1098, three years after Pope Urban II's initial call to arms, the Crusaders proceeded to Jerusalem, the location of the Holy Sepulcher of Jesus's resurrection. There they inflicted a terrible atrocity on the population, killing 40,000 inhabitants.[19] "The heaps of the dead presented an immediate problem for the conquerors," writes historian Christopher Tyerman in *God's War*. "Many of the surviving Muslim population were forced to clear the streets and carry the bodies outside the walls to be burnt in great pyres, whereat they themselves were massacred."[20] Jerusalem's Jews suffered a similar fate when they gathered in the main synagogue. The Crusaders "barricaded all the exits and stacked all the bundles of wood they could find in a ring around the building," writes historian Amin Maalouf. "The temple was then put to the torch. Those who managed to escape were massacred in the neighbouring alleyways. The rest were burned alive."[21]

For the Crusaders, killing Saracens—as all Muslims and some pagans were called—was a specifically religious duty, a path to heaven.[22] The Crusades were armed pilgrimages in which knights and their followers received forgiveness for their sins—and many of them were steeped in sins like theft and murder[23]—by undertaking a violent expedition endorsed by the pope. Violence and salvation were inextricably linked in the Crusader mind in a fashion inconceivable to the world of Islam at the time.

Christian atrocities were not confined to the Muslim adversary. Crusaders conducted major pogroms against Jews in Europe on their way to their holy land in the Middle East. "It seemed frankly illogical to most of the Crusaders to march thousands of miles to fight Muslims in the Middle East, about whom they knew very little, when the people who had actually killed Christ—or so they believed—were alive and well on their very doorsteps," writes theologian Karen Armstrong.[24] The money extorted or stolen from European Jews additionally helped to finance the expeditions to the Middle East.

Crusaders also killed Christians, lots of them, and it

wasn't just collateral damage. Several Crusades directly targeted the great Christian rival of Byzantium, which formally broke from Rome in 1054. During the Second Crusade, the crusader Reynaud conducted a rampage against Orthodox Christians on the island of Cyprus in 1156, a feat later overshadowed in the Third Crusade when Richard the Lionhearted returned to the island in 1191 to inflict an even greater devastation. But perhaps the most infamous of Crusader atrocities took place against Constantinople, the capital of Byzantium, in 1203. "For three days and nights, the Crusaders murdered, raped, looted, or destroyed everyone and everything they could get their hands on. Untold thousands perished; many more were brutalized, maimed, left homeless," writes Colin Wells in *Sailing from Byzantium.* "In the great church of Hagia Sophia . . . looters stripped the silken wall hangings, smashed the icons, tore apart the gold and silver furnishings, and then brought mules inside to load with booty. Some of the mules slipped and fell, unable to regain their footing on the blood-slicked marble floor."[25]

The Orthodox were not the only Christians put to the sword during the Crusades. During the Fourth Crusade, before they brutalized Constantinople, the Crusaders famously sacked the Catholic city of Zara—located in present-day Croatia. Only a few years later in 1209, Pope Innocent III declared the first official Crusade against fellow Christians, the heretics of Languedoc in southern France. In one particularly famous battle, the Crusaders surrounded the town of Beziers, a stronghold of the Albigensian heretics. When asked by the Crusaders prior to the attack how they might distinguish between the real Christians and the false ones, the papal legate replied, "Kill them [all]. God will know his own."[26] The Crusaders proceeded to kill every single man, woman, and child in the city, 20,000 in all, much as Saul killed the Amalekites. Not long after, Christendom would launch its first formal Inquisition, against the very same Albigensians, thus linking the two traditions: the war against the enemy without and the war against the enemy within.

One could use this short summary of Crusader cruelty to argue that Christianity is a uniquely intolerant and violent religion that has, despite the explicit teachings of Jesus but certainly in keeping with the Book of Revelations, conducted an unbroken stretch of atrocities against its perceived enemies at home and abroad. But the Crusaders claimed on the contrary that the Saracens were the uniquely and intrinsically cruel party—even though the bloodbaths that took place in Jerusalem, Constantinople, and the island of Cyprus stood in stark contrast to the history of Muslim conquest during this period. Four hundred years before the Crusaders drowned Jerusalem in blood, Caliph 'Umar conducted no slaughters when he took over the city. Indeed, he even signed a pact with the Christian patriarch Sophronius that pledged, according to Qur'anic teaching, "no compulsion in religion." Later, when the famous Muslim leader Saladin retook Jerusalem from the Crusaders in 1187, he likewise followed the example of 'Umar, not only allowing the Christian patriarch to leave the city along with his followers but permitting them to bring their riches with them.[27]

The Muslim world's relationship with Jews was even more of a contrast. While Crusaders conducted pogroms in Europe and targeted Jewish populations in the Middle East, Muslim leaders went out of their way to cultivate good ties with the Jewish world. From the beginning, Muslims allowed Jews to worship freely and live peaceably. Indeed, when Saladin invited Jews back to Jerusalem after retaking the city, he inspired a kind of early Zionism as Jews from all over the world streamed back to the region.[28]

Muslim leaders and military men committed their share of atrocities, both during the initial decades of conquest after the birth of the religion and in the later medieval period. But Muslims showed few of the genocidal impulses of their fellow monotheists. And the violence perpetrated by Muslims during the first 200 years of the Crusades was largely reactive. By the thirteenth century, when the soldier-slaves known as the Mamelukes seized control of the caliphate, writes Armstrong, "finally it looked as though the Christians had reproduced the murderous cruelty and hatred that they had felt for the Muslims in the hearts of the Muslims themselves."[29] In 1291, for instance, the Mamelukes sacked Acre and slaughtered everyone inside the city, a disturbing echo of what the Crusaders did in Jerusalem 200 years before.[30] Although the Qur'an tries to split the difference between the Old and New Testament teachings on retribution—"Let evil be rewarded with like evil. But he that forgives and seeks reconcilement shall be rewarded by Allah"[31]—the Mamelukes elevated vengeful-ness to a governing principle.[32]

The point here is not to deny Muslim violence or in-sist on the irrevocable murderousness of Christianity or Judaism. Rather, all three major monotheistic religions have a tradition of violence. And all three have traditions of tolerance. But the Crusaders projected onto Islam an intolerant violence that justified their own holy rampages, a trick of psychological jujitsu employed as well by our modern-day crusaders.

A corollary to the myth of the inherently violent Muslim is the myth of the inherently uncivilized Muslim. Crusaders imagined that they were engaged in a millennial battle between the forces of barbarism (Islam) and the forc-es of civilization (Christianity). But in fact, the Crusaders encountered a civilization more advanced in science, medi-cine, literature, economy, and philosophy. Even Arab farm-ers, who excelled at irrigation, cotton and silk production, and citrus cultivation, put European peasants to shame.[33] At that time, Islam was a truly global civilization, having encountered China long before Marco Polo and benefited greatly from Chinese inventions. In the ninth century, the Baghdad of Harun al-Rashid had a postal service, a sewage system, a free hospital, and several banks with branches as far away as China.[34] Palermo, the capital of Muslim Sicily, was one of the great cities of the world until the marauding Normans put a stop to that in 1072.[35] The Islamic world boasted universities in Cairo and Fez a full century before Europe managed something comparable.

Christian Europe was the backwater, just as it had been when Charles the Hammer stopped the Muslim advance at the French city of Tours in 732.[36] Medieval Europeans knew virtually nothing about the Greek and Roman literature that captivated Muslim thinkers. Indeed, from the Muslim point of view, the Crusaders were armored monsters who engaged in every uncivilized behavior up to and including cannibalism. "In Ma'arra our troops boiled pagan adults in cooking pots," admits Christian chronicler Radulph of Caen. "They impaled children on spits and devoured them grilled."[37] Inspired to fight by the largely imaginary atrocities conjured up by Pope Urban II, the Crusaders went on to commit real atrocities of their own. Nor did the behavior of the Crusaders improve over the years. Their destruction of Alexandria in 1365, which ironically coincided with the early stirrings of the Renaissance in Italy, was yet another victory of barbarism over civilization.[38]

Given this history, it is no surprise that the great Scottish philosopher David Hume called the Crusades "the most signal and most durable monument of human folly that has yet appeared in any age or nation."[39]

A Global Caliphate?

The myth of the inherently violent Muslim, which the Crusades burned into the very template of Western culture, is rivaled by the myth that Islam is bent on taking over the world. Indeed, the Crusaders justified their violence in order to forestall this horrific contingency. In a

1095 sermon, Pope Urban II reportedly declared, "This little portion of the world which is ours is pressed upon by warlike Turks and Saracens: for three hundred years they have held Spain and the Balearic Islands, and they live in hope of devouring the rest."[40]

In its early days, the expanding Islamic empire did indeed imagine an ever-growing *dar-al-Islam* (House of Islam). By the time of the Crusades, however, this initial burst of enthusiasm for expansion had long been spent. The Islamic world of the Iberian peninsula had already reached its limits, and the caliphate had lost its toehold in Italy. Conquest more often than not came at the expense of other Muslims, as when the Seljuks seized control of Jerusalem and other cities in the Holy Land from their Muslim rivals. So divided was the Muslim world at the time of the First Crusade that no one heeded the few calls to unite and retaliate for the sack of Jerusalem in 1099.[41] Still, scholars such as Bernard Lewis have persisted in the delusion that there was a "Muslim pincer grip on Europe" at the time of the Crusades.[42]

Moreover, the Christian West harbored its own desire to extend the pope's authority to every corner of the globe. The missionary impulse of Christianity has always been one of its strongest survival traits. Charlemagne pushed aggressively to convert as much of Europe as he could grasp. Forced conversion of Jews took place after the initial European pogroms of the First Crusade. Franciscan and Dominican missionaries set to work in the early thirteenth century to spread the faith in the Muslim world. That early believer in soft power, Francis of Assisi, sat down with Sultan al-Kamil during the Fifth Crusade with the aim of eliminating Islam through conversion.[43] Although the tolerance of Muslim rule during the Middle Ages has sometimes been exaggerated, people of various faiths did live more or less harmoniously. Christians and Jews, known as *dhimmis*, occupied second-class citizenship, but they were generally free to practice their religion and their profession as long as they paid their tax.

These two myths—of inherent violence and global ambitions—led to the firm conviction that Muslims were by nature untrustworthy. Robert of Ketton, a twelfth-century translator of the Qur'an, was typical in badmouthing the prophet Mohammed this way: "Like the liar you are, you everywhere contradict yourself." Crusaders frequently complained of the perfidy of their foe. For the thirteenth-century polemicist Fidentius, the crafty Muslim rulers routinely broke truces so that war, not negotiations, was the only answer.[44] The suspicion of untrustworthiness fell as well on any Christian who broached the possibility of coexistence with Islam. Pope Gregory IX, for instance, believed that the thirteenth-century Crusader Frederick II was himself the Antichrist because he developed close relationships with Muslims.

Perfidy, alas, was rather characteristic of the Crusaders themselves. For instance, during one of the more infamous German pogroms, the archbishop of Mainz promised to protect the town's Jews in exchange for silver, but then fled the scene, so that even the Jews sheltering in his palace were cut down.[45] In the sacking of Jerusalem in 1099, Crusaders killed a group of Muslims that the legendary Crusader Tancred himself had given sanctuary to in the al-Aqsa mosque.[46] In perhaps the most famous example, immortalized somewhat inaccurately on screen in Ridley Scott's 2005 film *Kingdom of Heaven*, the Crusader Reynauld of Châtillon broke the Christian truce with Saladin by attacking pilgrims on the *hajj*—the obligatory trip to Mecca—not once by twice.

In short, then, the picture of the Muslim handed down from the Crusades was overwhelmingly negative: violent, duplicitous, power-hungry, lustful. But at the same time, Muslims wrung a grudging respect from Christendom. Individual Saracens often won praise for their fighting spirit.[47] Saladin, the Kurdish leader who united the Muslim world and retook Jerusalem without massacre or bloodshed, emerged as a respected figure, even a chivalric hero. He appears in Limbo alongside Homer and Plato in Dante's *Inferno* (though Mohammed ends up in Hell as a "disseminator of scandal").

Later, this grudging respect dissipated with the rise of the Ottoman Empire, and stereotypes about Muslims remained strong. The "Turk" replaced the "Saracen" as the very antithesis of everything that Christian Europe represented. The capture of Constantinople in 1453, which marked the end of the Byzantine Empire and the disappearance of the official foothold that Christianity had in the Levant, was as cataclysmic a development for Europe as the Seljuk victories had been 400 years before. The

Turks were "mortal enemies" of European Christians, as Thomas More wrote, and Martin Luther too considered them, along with Roman Catholics, to be the Antichrist.[48] This anti-Turkish and anti-Muslim sentiment, as scholar Tomaz Mastnak points out, was central to the very first proposals for European union. Even the pacifist Quaker William Penn saw a chief virtue of his seventeenth-century plan for European integration in the "great security it will be to Christians against the inroads of the Turk."[49]

Only as the territorial threat of the Ottoman Empire faded did the political utility of these particular Muslim stereotypes lose their strength. As Muslim lands fell one by one to the colonial control of European powers, different stereotypes began to prevail: Muslims as backward and de-generate, lazing in their harems and tea shops. Like other Orientalists, the nineteenth-century French philosopher Ernest Renan portrayed the Muslim as "incapable of learn-ing anything or of opening himself to a new idea."[50] Yet, despite these perceptions of indolence and backwardness, scholars and activists in the Muslim world were very ac-tive during this period developing two primary responses to the depredations of colonialism: the secular nationalism that would find expression in Kemal Ataturk's transforma-tion of Turkey and the religious politics of Islamism that would eventually produce organizations like the Muslim Brotherhood. Only when Muslim actors again became powerful enough to challenge the colonial powers did the earlier Crusader myths, which had lain dormant but never disappeared, re-emerge.

The Myths Today

The disparagement of Muslims in the medieval literature was not simply a function of misinformation.[51] Rather the bias served a deep need. A Christian could not justify his own murderous practices unless they were somehow sanctified by the other's sins. According to Humbert of Romans in 1274, "the Muslims were culpable in the highest degree," observes one scholar of the period. "The church had the right to wield a sword against both heretics and rebels, and the Muslims were both."[52] Muslim sins justified Christian actions.

Similarly, the myths about Islam that circulate today reflect a deeper truth about the perceptions and anxieties of the fearful. We too must somehow justify our violence, and we look to our majors and our ministers for absolution. Islam "teaches violence," televangelist Pat Robertson proclaimed in 2005.[53] "The Koran teaches violence and most Muslims, including so-called moderate Muslims, openly believe in violence," declared Major General Jerry Curry (U.S. Army, ret.), who served in the Carter, Reagan, and Bush Sr. administrations.[54] Jerry Falwell, on *60 Minutes*, called Mohammed a "terrorist" and a "man of war" in contrast to Jesus and Moses.[55]

As during the Crusades, these characterizations of Islam have resonated at the highest ecclesiastical level. In 2006, Pope Benedict XVI began a speech at the University of Regensburg by quoting the aforementioned passage from Byzantine emperor Manuel II that speaks of Mohammed's legacy as "evil and inhuman" and citing his command to spread his faith "by the sword." Facing outraged protests from around the world, Pope Benedict apologized and said that his words were misunderstood.[56] But it wasn't the first time that the pope had distanced himself so clearly from his predecessor, Pope John Paul II, who had made great efforts to repair the breach between Christians, Jews, and Muslims.[57] "Not only has he questioned publicly whether Islam can be accommodated in a pluralistic society," journalist Christopher Caldwell writes approvingly of Benedict's stance. "He also demoted one of John Paul II's leading advisers on the Islamic world and tempered his support for a program of inter-religious dialogue run by Franciscan monks at Assisi."[58] Indeed Benedict has emerged as the Pope Urban II of his generation, promoting Christian proselytizing among Muslims and opposing Turkish membership in the European Union because it's not a Christian country.

Scholars too have perpetuated these core myths. The dean of Middle East studies, Bernard Lewis, made a splash in 1990 with an *Atlantic* article that fingered Islam itself, rather than colonialism or any other force external to the religion, as the primary source for "Muslim rage."[59] Lewis was later responsible for both the title and some of the more inflammatory content of his friend Samuel Huntington's best-selling book *The Clash of Civilizations*. "Muslim bellicosity and violence are late-twentieth century facts which neither Muslims nor non-Muslims can deny," Huntington wrote in his 1996 book, a sentiment that aptly describes the Crusader mentality of the eleventh century.[60]

Crusade 2.0 began as a response to the deplorable crimes of 9/11.[61] But the shock-and-awe violence of the modern-day crusade of the West is of a different magnitude than the terrorist massacres of September 11, 2001. The U.S.-led war on Iraq produced 25,000 civilian casualties in its first two years.[62] A 2006 study by U.S. and Iraqi epidemiologists estimated that more than 600,000 people died who would not have had the 2003 invasion never taken place.[63] The aerial bombing of Afghanistan killed more than a thousand civilians in 2002 alone, and another 3,000 people died as an immediate result of the impact of the war.[64] Thousands more have died in the ensuing years, and there have been many other civilian casualties in U.S. campaigns in Pakistan, Yemen, and elsewhere. In 2009, Harvard professor Stephen Walt calculated, conservatively, that the United States had killed nearly 300,000 Muslims over the last 30 years compared to only 10,000 U.S. fatalities at the hands of Muslims.[65]

The violence of Crusade 2.0, according to its apologists, has all been for worthy goals: ejecting the Taliban, dethroning Saddam Hussein, introducing democracy, guaranteeing the right of self-determination. "Our" violence has been instrumental, a regrettable means toward laudable ends that obscures other motives such as securing access to oil and natural gas. "Their" violence, on the other hand, results from their inherent iniquity and their millennial ambitions. "The ultimate goal of Islam is to rule the world," warns ex-Muslim Ali Sina.[66] Even the building of Park51 in lower Manhattan is presented as just another gambit in this age-old power grab: "This is Islamic domination and expansionism," writes right-wing blogger Pamela Geller, who made the "Ground Zero Mosque" into a media obsession.[67]

In the Islamophobic universe, it's not just al-Qaeda that wants to take over the world. According to this view, the Muslim Brotherhood has set up shop around the planet to infiltrate Western society, and the Saudi state has spent millions of dollars of its oil revenues to disseminate its version of Wahhabism, the notoriously intolerant eighteenth-century variant of Islam. But, as observers as politically divergent as Reza Aslan and Daniel Pipes agree, these actions constitute not a clash of civilizations but a clash *within* a civilization to which the West is largely an observer.[68] The Sunni Wahhabis are competing against rival interpretations of Islam, particularly the extremist al-Qaeda, Shi'ite Iran, and various offshoots of the Muslim Brotherhood. This is the real battle for the hearts and minds of Muslims, not the largely unsuccessful U.S.-led counterinsurgency efforts. Concludes foreign policy analyst William Pfaff, "The objectives of the Islamist movement are to purify Islam and the practices of Muslims and remove Western influence—not to conquer the West."[69]

On this issue of expansionism, we are again projecting our own anxieties upon our adversaries. The United States rejects the term "empire"—for that contradicts the republican ideals of the Founding Fathers—and yet we have struggled to sustain the "unipolar moment" in which we reign as sole superpower. The neoconservatives in the

Bush administration spoke with almost messianic fervor of promoting democracy in order to remap the Middle East along geopolitical lines more favorable to U.S. influence. Even more direct with their conversion aims were the Christian missionaries who rushed to the Middle East in the wake of the U.S. military, some of them explicitly invited to "do good" by an administration committed to faith-based charity. A new generation of these missionaries has been targeting the "10/40 window"—the huge swath of territory between the 40th parallel to the north and the 10th parallel to the south—which just happens to be home to the largest communities of Muslims.[70] In the U.S. military, too, a powerful faction promotes what whistle-blower Mickey Weinstein calls the "Talibanization" of the services, with the Officers' Christian Fellowship and their enlisted counterpart responding to Deputy Undersecretary of Defense for Intelligence William Boykin's infamous 2003 recruitment call for "warriors of God's kingdom."[71] The shock jocks on the home front speak an even cruder vernacular. "These people [Arabs and Muslims] need to be forcibly converted to Christianity," observes right-wing radio host Michael Savage. "It's the only thing that can probably turn them into human beings."[72]

Islamophobes have revived the notion that Muslims are inherently duplicitous, that they might seem to be engaged in inter-religious dialogue but are secretly plotting their take-over.[73] Consider the different interpretations of "Islamism." This term applies to anyone who, as analyst Graham Fuller defines it, "believes that Islam as a body of faith has something important to say about how politics and society should be ordered in the contemporary Muslim world and who seeks to implement this idea in some fashion."[74] Islamists of different political tendencies have formed parties to compete in elections all over the world. But the way Islamophobes use the term, Islamism has embedded within it all the stereotypes inherited from the Crusades. Algerian politician Said Sadi, for instance, argues that a "moderate Islamist is someone who does not have the means of acting ruthlessly to seize power immediately."[75] Violent, duplicitous, and power-hungry: he managed to hit all the clichés in seventeen words.

In the United States, meanwhile, Islamophobes presumed all Muslims to be guilty in the aftermath of 9/11: not just duplicitous but traitorous as well. "American Muslims must face their either/or," writes the novelist Edward Cline, "to repudiate Islam or remain a quiet, sanctioning fifth column."[76] Even American Muslims in high places like Congressman Keith Ellison have not been above suspicion. In a 2006 CNN interview with the Minnesota Democrat, Glenn Beck said, "I have been nervous about this interview with you, because what I feel like saying is, 'Sir, prove to me that you are not working with our enemies.'"[77] The onus, in other words, is on Muslims to prove that they are of the "good" variety rather than the "bad" variety. Many Americans have already made up their minds. According to one 2011 poll, one-third of Americans believe that Muslim-Americans are "not supportive" of the United States and are "too extreme" in their beliefs.[78]

To disseminate these myths, Islamophobes have revived other traditions from the Crusades era. It was common in the Middle Ages, for instance, to write scurrilous biographies of the prophet Mohammed.[79] Robert Spencer, the founder of JihadWatch, has updated the tradition with *The Truth about Muhammad: Founder of the World's Most Intolerant Religion*, which repeats all of the classic myths—about intolerance, about pedophilia—much as an anti-Jewish person would parrot that infamous forgery, *The Protocols of the Elders of Zion*.[80] Then there is the tradition of deliberately blaspheming Islam in order to provoke a violent response, as the Córdoba martyrs did in the ninth century by denouncing Mohammed in such public places as mosques during prayer times.[81] In our time, the burning of Qur'ans follows in this tradition of deliberate provocation, this time under the cover of free speech.

The myths of Islamophobia concerning the inherent violence, treachery, and global ambitions of Islam flourish in our era just as they did almost a millennium ago. In their cunning conflation of a certain type of Islamic radicalism with Islam itself, these myths have provided a language and an imagery for today's Islamophobia. According to this dynamic, the West rationalizes its own atrocities by emphasizing the hostile intent and inherent guilt of the presumed adversary.

But current anti-Islamic sentiment is not simply the Crusades warmed over. The political impetus for Crusade 2.0 comes from a Manichean conflict of a more recent vintage.

TWO

Islam: The New Communism

In 1951, the CIA and the emerging anticommunist elite, including soon-to-be-president Dwight Eisenhower, created the Crusade for Freedom as a key component of a growing psychological warfare campaign against the Soviet Union and its East European satellite. The language of this "crusade" was intentionally religious. It reached out to "peoples deeply rooted in the heritage of western civilization" but who were also living under the "crushing weight of a godless dictatorship."[1] In its call for the liberation of the communist world, it echoed the nearly thousand-year-old crusader rhetoric of recovering Jerusalem and other outposts of Christianity. These were both civilizational wars.

In America's Cold War theology, the Soviet Union replaced the Islamic world as the threatening infidel. However unconsciously, the old crusader myths about Islam translated remarkably easily into governing assumptions about the communist enemy: the Soviets and their allies were bent on taking over the world, could not be trusted with their rhetoric of peaceful coexistence, and therefore imperiled Western civilization. They also fought with unique savagery—think of the Chinese "hordes" during the Korean War—and a willingness to martyr themselves for the greater ideological good.

Some analysts made the explicit connection. Communism, French sociologist Jules Monnerot argued in the 1940s, was the new Islam. Both were religions. And both were totalitarian in nature, in the sense that they aspired to subject the individual to total control, had "a detailed plan for social order," and embraced "an egalitarianism in theory that often becomes oppression in practice."[2] In the mid-1950s, Bernard Lewis offered a similar assessment. Both Islam and communism "profess a totalitarian doctrine, with complete and final answers to all questions on heaven and earth," he wrote in an influential essay. "The answers are different in every respect, alike only in their finality and completeness, and in the contrast they offer with the eternal questioning of Western man."[3] Even though the Marxist ideology issued from the Western tradition, Communists were just like Muslims in their contempt for individualism.

Academic arguments were one thing, geopolitical realities quite another. The pragmatically oriented U.S. government in fact perceived Islam as an ally against godless communism during the Cold War. In 1957, a commission created by Eisenhower concluded that "Islam and Christianity have a common spiritual base in the belief that a divine power governs and directs human life and aspirations while communism is purely atheistic materialism."[4] Indeed, countries with a Muslim majority—Iran,

Saudi Arabia, Egypt, Turkey, Pakistan—would emerge as key allies against communism. Even before World War II came to a close, Franklin Roosevelt met secretly with King Abdul-Aziz ibn Saud to conclude an agreement granting Washington access to Saudi Arabian oil in exchange for a promise to respect the sovereignty of the king's new country.[5] Washington also cultivated close ties with Turkey, which it brought into NATO in 1952, and worked subsequently to bind Iran, Iraq, Pakistan, and Turkey in the Central Treaty Organization to prevent Soviet expansion into the Middle East.

This was not enough. Washington was so obsessed with its new crusade against communism that, on the theory that my enemy's enemy is my friend, it nurtured radical Islam as an additional weapon during the Cold War. As journalist Robert Dreyfuss ably details in his book *Devil's Game*, the U.S. funding of the mujahideen in Afghanistan after the Soviet Union's 1979 invasion was only the most well-known part of the anticommunist crusade in the Islamic world.[6] To undermine Arab nationalists and leftists who might align themselves with the Soviet Union, the United States worked with Iranian mullahs and facilitated the spread of the Muslim Brotherhood. In 1962, for instance, the United States used the Brotherhood in an effort to overthrow a pro-Nasser regime in Yemen.[7] Even Saudi proselytism met with favor in Washington. "Saudi efforts to Islamicize the region were seen as powerful and effective and likely to be successful," Dreyfuss quotes a CIA official. "We loved that. We had an ally against communism."[8]

Two events in 1979 transformed U.S. flirtation with Sunni extremists inspired by Saudi Wahhabism into a solid marriage of convenience. In Iran, Ayatollah Khomeini rode a wave of Shi'ite radicalism to overthrow the U.S.-backed Shah of Iran. Then, at the very end of the year, the Soviet Union invaded Afghanistan. To counterbalance Shi'ite Iran and defeat the Russians, the United States began funneling weapons to the mujahideen—"those who do *jihad*"—who were a mix of foreign and indigenous Muslim fighters. Washington even brought some of these fighters to train with the Green Berets and Navy SEALs at facilities in the United States.[9] When the Soviet Union fell apart in 1991, the U.S. government no longer needed the mujahideen. The marriage of convenience between Sunni extremists and the U.S. government dissolved, and *jihad* again became a bad word as Osama bin Laden and his band of former mujahideen gradually turned their attention to their next superpower target.

Although the Cold War ended in Europe in 1991, many of its concepts would live on, though the terms had become suddenly reversed. Where communism resembled the once-powerful Islam, in Monnerot's analysis of the 1940s, suddenly Islam began to resemble the once-powerful communism. Where analysts once spoke of a convergence between communism and fascism, they now spoke of a convergence between Islam and fascism. Where policy makers once held their noses to team up with Islamists against communists, now they made common cause with other unlikely allies to battle their former Islamist allies.

And after fifty years of ascribing violence, duplicity, and imperial ambitions to the communists, the West tailored these concepts once again to fit their original Crusades-era target: Muslims.

In Search of the Next Big Enemy

The Soviet threat justified an unprecedented expansion of the U.S. national security apparatus and the U.S. military budget. Because of the Soviet Union, the United States poured money into Europe, Japan, and South Korea to rebuild their war-torn societies, fought major conflicts in Korea and Vietnam, and waged countless proxy wars across the Third World. The very structure of U.S. power in the world rested on an anticommunist rationale: to lead and protect the Free World.

The collapse of the Cold War system left the United States in a unique global position of power with an extensive network of overseas bases, a huge military budget that sustained a Pentagon bureaucracy and myriad domestic manufacturers, and a diplomatic outlook nurtured by a tradition of exceptionalism. Adversaries remained. But no country posed a global challenge, and, frankly, none offered even a regional threat. Talk of "imperial overstretch"—inspired by historian Paul Kennedy's 1987 book *The Rise and Fall of Great Powers*—was quickly replaced by the triumphalism of the "end of history" as the United States celebrated its "unipolar moment."[10] But this very phrase produced a nagging anxiety, for a "moment" can be fleeting. How could the United States avoid irrelevance, isolationism, or, in the worse-case scenario of the emerging neoconservative movement, a tepid internationalism? Foreign policy elites in Washington began to sound almost nostalgic for the days of a clarifying adversary. The search for such an adversary was on. "The ideal enemy for America," wrote political scientist Samuel Huntington, "would be ideologically hostile, racially and culturally different, and militarily strong enough to pose a credible threat to American security."[11]

As a result of Iraq's invasion of Kuwait in 1990 and the subsequent U.S. counterattack in 1991, Saddam Hussein emerged as an enemy that could potentially sustain this unipolar moment. "How do you show the world that you're still a superpower?" observes Middle East analyst Phyllis Bennis. "You don't announce it at a press conference. No, you go to war. You go to war against Saddam Hussein."[12] The Iraqi dictator called on the world's Muslims to wage *jihad* against the Western invaders, but as with similar calls during the First Crusade, the Muslim world did not band together. Indeed, most Muslim countries (Saudi Arabia, Egypt, Pakistan) sided with Washington. The United States, too, stopped short of a full crusade by not proceeding to Baghdad and dethroning Hussein. In its construction of a "new world order," the George H.W. Bush administration showed other signs of reticence as well. It withdrew nuclear weapons from Korea, tried to pressure Israel into compromising in the Middle East, and stayed out of the Yugoslav wars. Hawkish critics fretted that the unipolar moment might be passing.

The Clinton administration tried something different. It initially proposed an "assertive multilateralism" and some version of a peace dividend that shifted resources from the military sector to civilian use. But the fiasco of U.S. military intervention in Somalia, the hesitation to respond to the Rwandan genocide, and disagreements with Europe over what to do in disintegrating Yugoslavia prompted a rethink on the multilateralism front. The administration ultimately did an about-face and reverted to knee-jerk unilateralism. It ended up rejecting key international treaties, undertaking military actions in Iraq and Kosovo without UN approval, pushing hard on military exports, and, in general, insisting that the United States was, as Secretary of State Madeleine Albright put it, an "indispensable nation." The "ideal enemy" of the period was the "rogue state." As political scientist Robert Littwak explained at the time, "The Clinton administration's rogue-state policy takes a disparate group of states—North Korea, Iran, Iraq, Libya, and Cuba—and essentially demonizes them for purposes of political mobilization."[13] But the U.S. public was unenthusiastic about Washington adopting the mantle of world's cop to confront every rogue and prevent every humanitarian disaster.[14] The emerging neoconservative movement, meanwhile, urged a more vigorous pursuit of "monsters to destroy," as William Kristol and Robert Kagan argued in an anti-Clinton broadside in *Foreign Affairs*. "Having defeated the 'evil empire,' the United States enjoys strategic and ideological predominance," they wrote. "The first objective of

U.S. foreign policy should be to preserve and enhance that predominance."[15]

For those looking for an enemy worthy of the United States, which could justify enormous military expenditures and heightened vigilance on the home front, one threat lurking on the horizon looked more promising than certifiable rogues like Serbia's Slobodan Milosevic or Iraq's Saddam Hussein. Al-Qaeda, "the base" that Osama bin Laden founded in Afghanistan in 1988, traced its lineage to Sayyid Qutb, an Egyptian militant who favored the use of violence to reestablish an Islamic caliphate.[16] Al-Qaeda was not happy with the way certain Middle Eastern governments had cozied up to the United States. It was particularly furious at U.S. troops setting up bases in Saudi Arabia, the sacred land of pilgrimage, as part of the first Gulf War.[17] Nor was it very happy with Islamist groups like the Muslim Brotherhood that were endorsing participation in democratic elections. Al-Qaeda launched its first major attack against Western targets with the first World Trade Center bombing in 1993. The embassy bombings in Kenya and Tanzania followed in 1998 and then the attack on the USS *Cole* in Aden in October 2000.

Al-Qaeda's ideology promised a militancy far more bracing than communism, though its aspirations still far exceeded its logistical capacity. Al-Qaeda was destructive, but tiny. Islam, on the other hand, was huge.

The emergence of Islam as the new "big enemy" was somewhat slow in coming. Bernard Lewis, in his 1990 essay "The Roots of Muslim Rage," acknowledged that although Islam was a formidable adversary, this "Muslim rage" had not fully engaged the United States: "There is no Cuba, no Vietnam, in the Muslim world, and no place where American forces are involved as combatants or even as 'advisers.'"[18] Daniel Pipes, who would later emerge as one of the chief ideologues who played up the new Islamic threat, wrote in a *National Review* article published a year after the fall of the Berlin Wall that terrorism and lack of democracy in the Muslim world troubled him, but "none of this justifies seeing Muslims as the paramount enemy."[19] Head of the CIA R. James Woolsey, another future mover of the Islamophobic agenda, concurred in 1994: "we should not accept the notion that the 'Red Menace' that dominated our lives for nearly a half a century is now being replaced by a 'Green Menace' sweeping throughout the Arab world."[20]

The few voices that called for a new crusade were tentative. In a 1990 editorial, the *Times* of London opined that "almost every month the threat from the Warsaw Pact diminishes; but every year, for the rest of this decade and beyond, the threat from fundamentalist Islam will grow."[21] In 1995, NATO Secretary General Willy Claes announced that "Islamic fundamentalism is at least as dangerous as Communism was."[22] But the uproar that greeted his remarks led to a quick retraction.[23] The following year, Elaine Sciolino showcased the debate over the Islamic threat in the *New York Times Magazine* but didn't come down on one side or the other.[24]

What was missing was a systematic way of understanding the new enemies of the post–Cold War period. In a 1993 issue of *Foreign Affairs*, Samuel Huntington published "The Clash of Civilizations" that described a new "pattern of conflict" for world politics, a set of fault lines that rearranged the world into a new map. History was not ending, he argued, but nation-states would not be responsible for the new types of conflicts engulfing the planet. The struggles of the twenty-first century would pit the great civilizations against each other: Western, Confucian, Japanese, Hindu, Slavic-Orthodox, Latin American, possibly African. But it was the Islamic civilization that posed the greatest threat for it possessed "bloody borders" wherever it abutted other traditions.[25] Although Huntington's thesis suffered from numerous flaws—many conflicts in the post–Cold War period, for instance, were *within* not *between* his so-called civilizations—it became an influential way of looking at the world, particularly the Muslim world.

The building blocks were in place. According to an emerging Islamophobic consensus, Muslims were angry, very angry, and this anger came from within their tradition rather than from decades of domination at the hands of colonial powers or forced secularization by reformers like Kemal Ataturk in Turkey. The Islamic civilization was inherently violent and posed a cultural challenge to the West, and organizations like al-Qaeda had even attacked U.S. targets overseas. To qualify as an enemy of the first rank, this emerging adversary just needed to prove that it could, as in the Middle Ages, directly threaten Western territory and its sacred sites.

The Rise of "Islamofascism"

On September 11, 2001, al-Qaeda went from being *a* threat to being *the* threat. Though it was a small outfit, didn't possess weapons of mass destruction or valuable territory, and was marginal even within the world of political Islam, al-Qaeda managed to command the attention of the United States like no other challenger in the post–Cold War era. What it lacked in conventional power, it made up for in audacity by launching an attack on U.S. soil—against the premier symbols of Western economic and military power. With this one act, it managed to turn Islam once again into an existential threat to the West.

The initial target of the George W. Bush administration after September 11 was not Islamic extremists *per se* but terrorism. The "global war on terror" was a vague phrase that not only suffered from being a category error—it was impossible to wage war on a technique or against a non-state actor—but could equally apply to other groups on the U.S. list of terrorist organizations such as Basque Fatherland and Liberty or on its list of state sponsors of terror like Cuba. Many right-wing observers were not happy with this loose phrase because it didn't finger Islam or even radical Islam.[26]

In his 2002 State of the Union address, Bush tried out a different approach: the infamous phrase "axis of evil" that linked Iraq, Iran, and North Korea, the last thrown in to preempt charges of Islamophobia. The original proposal from speechwriter David Frum had been "axis of hatred," but his colleague Michael Gerson, an evangelical

Christian, wanted something more theological. As Frum explains further, the term "axis" was designed to conjure up images of fascism. "Much as they quarreled with each other, Iraq, Iran, Hezbollah and al-Qaida shared beliefs that harked back to European fascism: Disdain for free inquiry and rational thought, a celebration of death and murder, and obsessive anti-Semitism," he wrote. "They all resented the power of the West, and they all despised the humane values of democracy."[27] The "axis of evil" was an important intermediary term between the "global war on terror" (GWOT) introduced in the immediate aftermath of the attacks and the later embrace of "Islamofascism." Its fusion of the theological and the geopolitical captured the essence of Crusade 2.0.

Eventually the Bush administration would try to reframe the conflict once again. In 2005, public support for U.S. involvement in Iraq was fading. Bush needed a framework that could make sense of his foreign policy. He needed a threat big enough and durable enough, with Saddam Hussein gone and the 9/11 attacks retreating into memory, to justify American sacrifices: soldiers lost, money spent, civil liberties abridged, and critical issues such as climate change and China's rise ignored. In an October 2005 speech at the National Endowment for Democracy (NED), the president introduced the term "Islamofascism" into the presidential discourse. Rather than simply being a handful of evildoers hiding out in caves somewhere along the Afghan-Pakistan border, Islamofascism was a civilizational threat comparable to the Soviets, an enemy that required national mobilization.

"The murderous ideology of the Islamic radicals is the great challenge of our new century," Bush said in the NED speech. "Yet in many ways, this fight resembles the struggle against communism in the last century." He went on to enumerate the similarities: both communists and Islamofascists were elitist, had a "cold-blooded contempt for human life," and pursued "totalitarian aims."[28]

The linking of Islam and fascism was not new. Historians had explored the connections between Muslims and Nazis before and during World War II.[29] The Baath movement—which produced ruling parties in Iraq and Syria—had roots in earlier fascist movements. When scholar Malise Ruthven coined the phrase "Islamo-fascism" in a 1990 article, he had in mind dictatorial governments, some of which were allied with the United States, like Pakistan and Morocco.[30] Newt Gingrich later played around with the term "totalitarian Islam" to describe Iran.[31] After 9/11, however, writers like Christopher Hitchens and academics like Bassam Tibi redeployed the term "Islamofascism" to describe the Islamist opposition to those dictatorial governments. Suddenly, it was no longer just al-Qaeda that was "totalitarian," but a whole group of Islamists who constituted something like the all-encompassing Soviet state and system.[32] For instance, the Muslim Brotherhood, according to Tibi, aspired to fuse religion and state into a global system demanding total allegiance through an Islamic variant of Trotsky's "permanent revolution," Stalin's instrumental internationalism, and Lenin's vanguardism.[33] This union of anticommunism and Orientalism offered a view of political Islam as unitary and opaque, with operatives as hidebound, fanatical, and incapable of change as the communists were once assumed to be.[34] Here, finally, was Huntington's "ideal enemy," not just a few al-Qaeda radicals but millions of Islamofascists, all marching in lock step.

Once President Bush finally embraced the rhetoric of Islamofascism, the hard right shifted into overdrive. In his book *World War IV*, Norman Podhoretz, the publisher of *Commentary* magazine, urged his readers to rise to the new challenge just as the greatest generation took on fascism and their children confronted the Soviet Union.[35] Like Pope Urban II summoning the first Crusaders, Podhoretz implied that the battle was even more epic than anything that had come before, a confrontation of truly biblical proportions with an adversary of between 125 and 200 million people that outnumbered all the fascists and communists who had ever lived (given the population of China alone, this was truly an odd assertion).[36] For Daniel Pipes, who was finally getting around to seeing Islam as the paramount enemy, the threat was much worse than what communism offered because communists only disagreed with Western politics whereas Islamists "despise the entire Western way of life."[37]

The "Islamofascism" school—which also includes Donald Rumsfeld, David Horowitz, Bill O'Reilly, and Pamela Geller—treats the Islamic world as a modern Communist International where Arab governments and radical

Islamists work hand in glove. Absent is any appreciation that the Syrian, Egyptian, and Saudi Arabian governments have launched their own attacks on radical Islam. The sharp divides between the Iranian regime and the Taliban, between the Jordanian government and the Palestinians, between Shi'ites and Sunni in Iraq, and even among Kurds all disappear in the totalitarian blender, just as anticommunists generally failed to distinguish between the communist hardliner Leonid Brezhnev and the communist reformer Mikhail Gorbachev. This fundamental misunderstanding of the world of Islam unfortunately extends beyond the far right.

Jihad Liberals

Conservatives and liberals once waged the Cold War together. Democrats like Harry Truman, John F. Kennedy, and Lyndon Johnson joined with their conservative colleagues to pursue the containment of the Soviet Union and China, the rollback of perceived threats in Korea and Vietnam, and large-scale increases in budgets for the Pentagon and intelligence community. The failures of the Vietnam War fractured this liberal-conservative consensus, as liberals began to oppose the war and a hard right began to question Richard Nixon and Henry Kissinger's *realpolitik* engagement with Russian and Chinese communism. From this broken consensus emerged the neoconservative movement, which linked hawkish Democrats and Republicans who disliked détente and the "Vietnam syndrome" constraints on U.S. power.

Some liberals, too, eventually sought to exorcise the ghosts of Vietnam by attempting to recover the "fighting spirit" of Truman. They supported humanitarian interventions during the Clinton era to beat back aggressors like Slobodan Milosevic in Serbia and warlords in Somalia. After 9/11, the writer Michael Ignatieff took to calling this new muscular liberalism "empire lite," for it relied on overwhelming U.S. military force not to create dependent colonies but rather to build new nations out of chaos and save threatened populations from genocide.[38] These rebranded liberals, many of whom supported the U.S. invasion of Iraq in 2003 because it deposed an authentic tyrant, put the struggle against injustice, if necessary by military means, at the center of their thinking. Since this empire-lite approach corresponds with the external struggle of the lesser *jihad* of Islam—not to be confused with the greater *jihad* that involves an internal effort to master one's desires—Ignatieff and other such thinkers are best described as *jihad* liberals.

Take the case of Peter Beinart, the former *New Republic* editor. His 2006 book *The Good Fight* was a literal call to arms for liberals and progressives. By invoking the older generation of Cold War liberals who crafted their muscular philosophy in the struggle against communism, Beinart urged his fellow liberals, who had grown complacent and even isolationist in their instincts, to join the fight against the "totalitarian movement" of "jihadist terrorism."[39] If Serbian aggression in Bosnia in the 1990s justified the overriding of the traditional progressive resistance to U.S.

military intervention, the Taliban and Salafists offered an even stronger rationale to fight in the twenty-first century.[40] This threat prompted Beinart to support the U.S. invasion of Iraq and the larger fight against Islamofascism. "In the liberal vision," he writes, "there is no contradiction between recognizing that our enemies are not intrinsically evil, and recognizing that they must be fought, just as there is no contradiction between recognizing that although we are not intrinsically good, we must still fight them."[41]

For other *jihad* liberals like Paul Berman, the enemy is indeed intrinsically evil. In both *Terror and Liberalism* (2003) and *The Flight of the Intellectuals* (2010), Berman sketches out a genealogy of evil, from Muslim collaboration with the Nazis and Palestinian suicide bombers to Saddam Hussein's megalomaniacal tyranny and al-Qaeda's death cult.[42] That Hussein had no connection to al-Qaeda, that al-Qaeda's dream of a caliphate did not jibe with the Palestinian state constructed by Hamas, that Saudi Arabia feared bin Laden as much as the United States did, none of this mattered, any more than the doctrinal differences between Moscow and Beijing did for hard-core cold warriors. The intrinsic evil of each element qualified its inclusion in Berman's catch-all category of Islamofascism, which he defines as the antithesis of liberal values.[43]

In Berman's theology, the devil doesn't come in a sulfurous cloud brandishing a pitchfork or dressed in a suicide vest. Rather, the object of Berman's most assiduous attacks, Swiss-born Muslim scholar Tariq Ramadan, is urbane, academic, and dressed in a suit. Since it is not so obvious that Ramadan is a representative of Islamo-fascism, Berman must work hard to expose him. He deconstructs Ramadan's past and prose to demonstrate that, after all, the scholar embodies all the worst qualities of his religion: violence, treachery, and imperial ambition. Because Ramadan's father and grandfather were instrumental in establishing the Muslim Brotherhood, Ramadan too must at some essential level ascribe to the same belief system. This becomes somewhat difficult given Ramadan's explicit condemnation of terrorism. So Berman constructs a syllogism that would have met the high standards of the Inquisition: "1) Ramadan condemns terrorism. 2) He wants to understand terrorism, though not to justify it. 3) He understands terrorism so tenderly that he ends up justifying it. 4) He justifies it so thoroughly that he ends up defending it."[44] Berman simply ignores Ramadan's denunciations of anti-Semitism. And when he can't find evidence for any of his claims that Ramadan is a closet extremist, Berman indulges in pure conjecture: "The combination of these several tones, the affectless and the furious, makes you wonder yet again—makes me, at least, wonder—if some quirk in his thinking hasn't been conveniently hidden from sight. A theory about conspiratorial Jews, maybe? A few ideas concerning terrorism?"[45] This is a witch-hunt world where, as journalist Stephan Salisbury puts it, "absence of evidence is evidence itself."[46] It doesn't matter what Muslims say because, according to the old Crusade myth, they are inherently untrustworthy. As writer Arun Kundnani observes, "Whatever a 'moderate

Islamist' argues, the outcome is always the same—support for Hamas, if not al-Qaida."[47]

Like their ultra-conservative cousins, *jihad* liberals of the secular fundamentalist variety don't bother with fine distinctions. They dispense with tolerance in the social sphere much as Berman and Beinart dispensed with caution in the foreign policy arena. "We are not fighting a 'war on terror,'" writes Sam Harris, the author of several books promoting atheism. "We are fighting a pestilential theology and a longing for paradise."[48] Comrade-in-arms Richard Dawkins indulges in similar Islamophobia with his labeling of the religion as a "great evil."[49] Alas, secularists can embody the crusading spirit as fully as their religious brethren. Like the Crusaders of old, they portray Islam as an inherently violent and unchangeable system that threatens "our" civilization.

Ironically, all this discussion about Islamofascism has been taking place at the same time that political Islam itself was undergoing a dramatic transformation. Just as right-wing activists and *jihad* liberals were trying to demonize political Islam as totalitarian and thus fixed in place like a fly in amber, the object of their worst fears was evolving faster than anyone ever anticipated.

Islam Modernizing

In 1989, revolutions spread through Eastern Europe and unseated communist regimes. The same winds of change blew away apartheid in South Africa and encouraged activists in China to gather in Tiananmen Square. The Muslim world was not immune to these developments. To stave off more radical demands, King Hussein in Jordan permitted the country's first semi-free elections in 1989 just days before the fall of the Berlin Wall. Islamists did well, even joining the cabinet. Three years later, the parliament legalized political parties. But King Hussein then backtracked on democratic reforms, and Jordan has been stuck politically ever since. The main opposition Islamic Action Front alleged vote-rigging by the government in 2007 and boycotted the 2010 elections.[50]

The Jordanian royal family, like other autocrats in the region, was worried about the other post-1989 political scenario in the Middle East: Algeria. In local elections in 1990, an Islamic party in Algeria won 62 percent of the vote. In the national elections the following year, the new party Front Islamique du Salut won more seats than any other. The Algerian government took a dim view of this democratic development, however. With French support, it banned the new party, threw its leaders in jail, and sent thousands of activists to detention camps in the Sahara desert. A civil war ensued that left more than 100,000 dead.[51]

The overturning of an election followed by gross human rights abuses would ordinarily have elicited a strong condemnation from Washington. Instead, the United States acquiesced to the changes, just as it did a couple years earlier when the Turkish military's "soft coup" of 1997 removed an Islamist prime minister. To avoid charges of anti-Islamic bias, U.S. officials couched their "Islamist exception" in universalist terms. The U.S. government opposed what it called "one person, one vote, one time."[52] In common parlance, this translated into a fear that Islamist parties would use democratic means to rise to power and then kick away the democratic ladder beneath them. Authoritarian governments in the region have repressed their Islamist oppositions knowing full well that the "Islamist exception" will protect them—but usually not repressing them out of existence since having a few Islamists on hand reminds Washington of the dangers of pushing too hard for democratic reforms.

The *idée fixe* that Islamists are the problem, not the authoritarian regimes running Middle Eastern countries into the ground, owes much to the Orientalist notion that Islam retards economic and political development. According to scholars like Bernard Lewis, Islam might have encouraged innovation in the Middle Ages, when the West was in its barbaric infancy, but in the modern age Islam has been the glass ceiling that prevents the rise of entrepreneurs and democrats alike.[53]

However inaccurate this contention might have been in the past, it was visibly nonsensical at the time of Crusade 2.0. Turkey has emerged as a vibrant democracy and a major foreign policy player. Indonesia, the world's most populous Muslim country, is now the largest economy in Southeast Asia and the eighteenth largest economy in the world. In both cases, Islam-influenced parties played key roles in the transformation. And once they won, they did not, as some feared, kick the democratic ladder out from underneath them. They played by the rules during the elections and have observed those rules once in power. "Since the early 1990s," writes Philip Howard in *The Digital Origins of Dictatorship and Democracy*, "23 Muslim countries have developed more democratic institutions, with fairly run elections, energized and competitive political parties, greater civil liberties, or better legal protections for journalists."[54]

Even organizations that the United States has maintained on its terrorism list, such as Hezbollah and Hamas, made the decision to engage in the political process. Both organizations played a key role in organizing civil society in Lebanon and Gaza. Both ultimately backed away from terrorism to focus instead on participation in the political process. Hezbollah first fielded candidates for political office in 1992 and has been represented in the Lebanese parliament ever since, even holding at various times several positions in the Lebanese government. Hamas, meanwhile, won parliamentary elections in 2006, took over governing of Gaza, and immediately faced a political boycott by Israel and the United States. It continues to maintain a military wing, but it has largely stopped its earlier campaign of suicide bombing and "approximately 90 percent of its work is in social, welfare, cultural, and educational activities," according to Israeli scholar Reuven Paz.[55] Like other organizations branded as terrorist—the Irish Republican Army, the African National Congress—both Hamas and Hezbollah used violence to achieve their goals but morphed into political entities when given an authentic opportunity to do so. As Geula Cohen, former member of the Jewish terrorist organization Lehi, put it, "Every movement for freedom throughout history was forced to use means of force, guns, and so on because when you are a minority, you can't fight the government face-to-face."[56] Lehi, otherwise known as the Stern Gang, eventually became part of the Israeli Defense Forces.

The Muslim Brotherhood, probably the most influential Islamist organization with chapters all over the world, has made a similar transformation, renouncing its earlier support of violence. The Brotherhood encompasses many different types of groups, write Robert Leiken and Steven Brooke in a 2007 *Foreign Affairs* article, but "all reject global jihad while embracing elections and other features of democracy."[57] As the Egyptian Brotherhood's 2004 Initiative for Reform reads, "Comprehensive reform cannot be achieved except by implementing democracy, which we believe in, and whose fundamentals we commit ourselves to."[58] The French scholar Gilles Kepel makes an apt comparison between the Brotherhood and the Eurocommunists of the 1970s, who broke with Soviet orthodoxy to participate in democratic elections and stake out a more neutral foreign policy.[59]

Those who work in Muslim communities are very clear about the distinction between political Islam and violent militants. In one particularly telling example, the British authorities worked with the Muslim Association of Britain (MAB), a Western offshoot of the Brotherhood, to take over the Finsbury Park mosque from the followers of Abu Hamza, an extremist Egyptian cleric. Robert

Lambert, the former head of the Muslim Contact Unit in the London Metropolitan Police and one of the master-minds of the MAB's takeover of the Finsbury Park mosque, "believes that only groups like MAB and even nonviolent Salafis have the street credibility to challenge the narrative of al-Qaeda and influence young Muslims."[60]

Political Islam, in other words, has been undergoing a major transformation. Although a smaller number of mili-tants continue to embrace terrorism, all the major Islamist forces have moved in the opposite direction. Meanwhile, the "Islamofascist" conflation of al-Qaeda and these move-ments of political Islam, two formations with antithetical goals, "has served only to strengthen those who want 'to burn down the system,'" as analyst Alistair Crooke has argued.[61]

Within the religion as well, ferment has been tak-ing place. Scholars such as Taha Husayn, Amin al-Khuli, and Ahmad Khalafalla have challenged the notion that the Qur'an is the literal word of God.[62] Imam Amina Wadud, professor and activist Ingrid Mattson, and Zainah Anwar of the Malaysian group Sisters in Islam have brought a feminist perspective to the practice of Islam. John Esposi-to, a specialist in Islam who was once in Catholic seminary, compares the changes taking place within Islam to the transformations inside Catholicism that culminated in the Second Vatican Council between 1962 and 1965. It was, Esposito recalls, a vanguard of reformers who made the difference. "In the Muslim world, there is a burgeoning group, a significant group but still a vanguard of Muslim religious reformers," he says. "It's not just older figures but also there's a younger generation who have been educated within their countries or in western countries where much of the thinking on religious pluralism has been going on."[63]

In the economic realm, too, the world of Islam has been changing rapidly. In Turkey, for instance, Islam was not only an important ingredient in political change. It was also at the heart of the country's economic surge at the outset of the twenty-first century. Istanbul became the center of a laboring, thinking, and creating class that faced both westward toward Europe and the United States and eastward toward the Middle East and Central Asia. Central Anatolia and its key city, Kayseri, once considered a Turkish backwater, had become a vital center of manufacturing. "While Anatolia remains a socially conservative and religious society, it is also undergoing what some have called a 'Silent Islamic Reformation,'" according to the European Stability Initiative's influential 2005 report on Turkey's new Islamic Calvinists. "Many of Kayseri's business leaders even attribute their economic success to their 'protestant work ethic.'"[64]

These political and economic changes have been accompanied and supported by the technological revolution. Muslims throughout the world tune in to al-Jazeera TV programs to get a much wider range of news and commentary than has traditionally been available. TV evangelists like Ahmad al-Shugairi in Saudi Arabia, Amr Khaled in Egypt, and Aa Gym in Indonesia have captured huge followings with their moderate messages.[65] The annual growth rate of Internet use in the Muslim world outstrips that of other developing countries, with the number of users on average doubling every eight months since 2000.[66] Twitter and Facebook have become essential tools of civic engagement up to and including the take-down of authoritarian regimes, as the Arab Spring has demonstrated.

Given this dramatic remaking of the Muslim world, the attacks of 9/11 appear to be a throwback to an earlier era rather than a harbinger of things to come. "The notion that an Islamic state should be created through holy war is an idea whose time has passed among most in the Muslim world," writes scholar Noah Feldman.[67] As the demonstrations that broke out in Egypt, Tunisia, and elsewhere in the Middle East in 2011 have suggested, Muslims are defying the "totalitarian" stereotype of their political mind-set to work toward their own versions of liberal democracy that have not been imposed from the outside or simply copied from Western models.

Bipolar Disorder

In the mid-1980s, the United States did not immediately respond to the changes taking place in the Soviet Union under Mikhail Gorbachev. It was extraordinarily difficult for policy makers who lived and breathed myths about Soviet expansionism to acknowledge that Gorbachev might have been implementing something remarkable with his *glasnost* and *perestroika*. At the CIA, Robert Gates had repeated run-ins with the State Department because of his skepticism about the genuine nature of Gorbachev's reforms.[68] The conservative foreign policy apparatus assumed that Gorbachev was practicing deception, trying to lure the United States into complacency before resuming its efforts to expand its power.[69]

This bipolar disorder continues to plague Washington's view of communism's replacement, Islamism. Policy makers resist looking at the evolution of political Islam, fail to distinguish between different varieties, and, in the worst-case scenario, impute "totalitarian" characteristics to what is proving to be a vital force for democratization in the Muslim world. The misconceptions of *jihad* liberals and their right-wing allies mirror al-Qaeda's lumping together of all the various forces in the infidel West. As during the Cold War, hardliners reinforce one another.

The persistence of Crusader myths and their transposition into a Cold War framework help explain why the West remains essentially clueless about Islam. These longstanding myths don't, however, fully explain the recent spike in Islamophobia in the United States after several years of relative quiescence. To understand this, we must turn to the third unfinished war: the global war on terror launched by George W. Bush after 9/11.

THREE

The Launch of Crusade 2.0

In the immediate aftermath of 9/11, it looked as though the Crusades were beginning again, quite literally. In a speech on the Sunday after the attack, President George W. Bush framed the conflict between the United States and its enemies as a war of good against evil. Then he uttered a phrase that made his European allies and Muslims around the world cringe. "This crusade, this war on terrorism, is going to take awhile," the president said. The use of the word "crusade" was "most unfortunate," lamented Soheib Bensheikh, grand mufti of the mosque in Marseille, France. "It recalled the barbarous and unjust military operations against the Muslim world."[1] It also recalled the rhetoric of al-Qaeda and its allies, which launched its "jihad against Jews and Crusaders" in 1998.[2]

The Bush administration immediately apologized for the reference. The president would use the word once more in a speech to U.S. and Canadian troops in Alaska, invoking an Eisenhower-like "crusade to defend freedom," but that would mark the end of explicit Crusade rhetoric.[3] Indeed, the Pentagon backed off its initial code name for the October 2001 invasion of Afghanistan—Operation Infinite Justice—for fear of offending the Muslim community by implying that the U.S. military, rather than Allah alone, could dispense such justice.[4]

The president went beyond these token gestures. In his speeches in the early days, he took pains to distinguish between Islam and the actions of al-Qaeda. "The terrorists practice a fringe form of Islamic extremism that has been rejected by Muslim scholars and the vast majority of Muslim clerics; a fringe movement that perverts the peaceful teachings of Islam," Bush said in his address to Congress on September 20, 2001.[5] This distinction between Islam as a religion and the actions of a few Muslims followed the model established by the Clinton administration in the 1990s.[6]

Meanwhile, anti-Islamic sentiment was rising dangerously. The American-Arab Anti-Discrimination Committee, on the day after 9/11, confirmed 30 reports of violent harassment.[7] The FBI was opening forty investigations into hate crimes against Arab-Americans. The Council on American-Islamic Relations reported 350 attacks in the week following 9/11.[8] There were at least five bias-related murders in the immediate aftermath of the attacks.[9]

In an important move, the president visited a mosque in Washington DC on the Monday after the attacks. He spoke out against the violence directed toward Muslim Americans: "Those who feel like they can intimidate our fellow citizens to take out their anger don't represent the best of America, they represent the worst of humankind and they should be ashamed of that kind of behavior."[10] This rhetoric and this action had more than simply symbolic value. "President Bush's appearance at the mosque saved many people's lives," a representative of a major national Arab American advocacy organization told researchers Anny Bakalian and Mehdi Bozorgmehr.[11] A presidential advisor told the researchers of his influence on the president: "I said, 'The president has to visit a mosque. You have to say 'churches, synagogues, and mosques.' When they say 'Judeo-Christian,' you should say, 'Christians, Muslims, and Jews.' So, if you noticed, Bush started that tradition."[12]

The administration reached out even further. U.S. officials gave more interviews to al-Jazeera in the two months after 9/11 than in all of the preceding years the network had been in Washington.[13] In October 2001, the State Department brought in advertising executive Charlotte Beers to head a new outreach initiative to the Muslim world as part of an effort to win the "hearts and minds" of Muslims globally.

But all of these discrete efforts to appeal to "good Muslims" and isolate "bad Muslims" ultimately ran up against the Bush administration's larger strategic campaign. The implementation of this campaign would indiscriminately stigmatize Muslims of all types and varieties, much as coalition forces after the fall of the Taliban in Afghanistan rounded up suspected Muslim militants as diverse and as unlikely as a 14-year-old Chadian national and a frail Afghan septuagenarian. Even as they placated Muslim Americans with speeches and mosque visits, the president, his advisors, and his speechwriters were beginning to frame the emerging conflict as more than just a fight against a small terrorist organization or the government of Afghanistan that harbored it. In the same speech to Congress in which he praised Islam as a peaceful religion, the president issued this warning: "Every nation, in every region, now has a decision to make. Either you are with us, or you are with the terrorists." This black-and-white division of the world recalled the bipolarism of the Cold War era and the theological certainties of the Crusades. The president left no middle ground for Muslims or anyone else who condemned the 9/11 attacks but opposed as well an increasingly militarized U.S. foreign policy.

The Bush administration might have treated the 9/11 attacks as a crime committed by the equivalent of a Mafia syndicate. Instead, it went to war. And those wars took place in Muslim lands. The plan, moreover, was not simply to punish Taliban for harboring al-Qaeda. Even the deposing of Saddam Hussein, who had nothing to do with 9/11, was only an intermediate goal. Vice President Dick Cheney, Pentagon chief Donald Rumsfeld, and other neoconservatives in the administration, who had been waiting for several decades for this chance to radically alter U.S. foreign policy, had a much more ambitious plan: to remap the Middle East. By toppling the dictator in Iraq—and then moving on to the regimes in Iran and Syria—they hoped to inspire a wave of democracy in the region and strengthen Israel's position with respect to its neighbors and the Palestinians. They were so intent on this plan that they disregarded the likelihood that elections in the region would, as in Algeria in 1991, enfranchise the very Islamists they feared.[14]

Today's Crusaders have much in common with their Crusade 1.0 counterparts. Their actions are shaped by a Manichean theology. Their adversaries are Muslims while their allies are primarily Christian. Their objective is to transform the Middle East, and their tactics are military. Their ultimate goals have turned out not to be the stated ones. And, perhaps most importantly, the stakes of both Crusade 1.0 and 2.0 have been the very highest. Civilization itself is at risk. And only a "global war on terror" against an "axis of evil" can save the West.

Finding a Precedent

The United States came along too late to be part of the Crusades. One of the New World's comparative advantages was the clean break it promised from the wars and religious intolerance of the Old World. In the aftermath of 9/11, as the U.S. government was assembling the various parts of a global war that would target Muslims at home and abroad, apologists for the effort hastened to provide examples of America's pro-Muslim bias. Founding Father Thomas Jefferson owned a Qur'an and showed every indication of having read it. The Clinton administration went to war to protect Bosnian and then Kosovar Muslims. American Muslims, meanwhile, enjoy freedom of religion, their level of household income is equal to or even a little better than average, and their acquisition of college degrees is twice the national average.[15] Those trying to reach Muslim hearts and minds worked hard to create the impression that the United States was and had always been a friend to Muslims everywhere.

But a counter-narrative promoted by preachers, politicians, and pundits asserted something quite different, that the discovery of America resulted from an anti-Muslim impulse, the country's central military institutions emerged from anti-Muslim battles, and the war on terror was not an aberration in U.S. history but a continuity. The Pentacostal preacher Rod Parsley, for instance, declared that "America was founded, in part, with the intention of seeing this false religion [Islam] destroyed."[16] This was no mere bluster from the pulpit. Columbus, whose "discovery" of indigenous-populated lands coincided with the expulsion of first Jews and then Muslims from his adopted country Spain, did indeed want to use the profits from the spice trade to battle Islam in India and eventually achieve that Holy Grail of the Crusades, the reconquest of Jerusalem.[17]

A clue to the second contention, concerning the anti-Muslim lineage of U.S. military institutions, can be found in the Marine Corps hymn, which begins "*From the halls of Montezuma to the shores of Tripoli.*" In 1801, the United States went to war against the nominally Muslim Barbary states of North Africa—Tripoli, Algiers, Tunis—because their pirates had been seizing U.S. vessels and taking seamen hostage. During this four–year battle against the Barbary pirates, the U.S. Marine Corps came into its own with a daring raid on the Tripolitan port of Derne. The lead-up to the war also spurred the first major U.S. government expenditures on a blue-water navy that could fight distant wars.[18] For historians like Robert Kagan, the Barbary Wars kicked off what would be a distinguished history of empire, which he contrasts with the conventional wisdom that the United States only reluctantly assumed its hegemonic mantle.[19]

The Barbary Wars were, for some, a useful precedent for a country about to embark on a "good war" against bad Muslims. Shortly after the September 11 attacks, law professor Jonathan Turley invoked the war against the Barbary pirates in congressional testimony to justify U.S. retaliation against Muslim terrorists.[20] Historian Thomas Jewett, conservative journalist Joshua London, and the executive director of the Christian Coalition of Washington State, Rick Forcier all pointed to those pirates as Islamic radicals *avant la lettre* to underscore the impossibility of negotiations and the necessity of war, both then and now.[21] Actually, religion played little role in the U.S. confrontation with the Barbary pirates, since the conflict was largely about access to trade.[22] The pirates, interested in booty above all, were hardly terrorists, and their slavery practices paled in comparison to U.S. practices at the time. In the end, the Barbary Wars didn't serve as much of a precedent for the post-9/11 retaliations.

There was, however, one interesting parallel: the use of suicide bombing. But it was the United States that introduced the tactic—on September 4, 1804. The U.S.

Navy was desperate to penetrate the enemy defenses in Tripoli. Commodore Edward Preble, who headed up the Third Mediterranean Squadron, chose an unusual stratagem: sending a booby-trapped USS *Intrepid* into the bay at Tripoli to destroy as many of the enemy's ships as possible. U.S. sailors packed 10,000 pounds of gunpowder into the boat along with 150 shells then volunteered to blow themselves up with the boat so as not to be captured and lose so much valuable gunpowder to the enemy. In the end, the explosion didn't do much damage—at most, one Tripolitan ship went down—but the crew was killed just as surely as the two men who plowed a ship piled high with explosives into the USS *Cole* in the Gulf of Aden nearly 200 years later. Despite the failure of the mission, Preble received much praise for his strategies, even from the pope. "The American commander, with a small force and in a short space of time, has done more for the cause of Christianity than the most powerful nations of Christiandom have done for ages!"[23] In this one act, the United States proved it could match the Europeans in the Crusade game.

The Bush administration did not directly invoke the Barbary Wars as it undertook Crusade 2.0.[24] The American public responded more positively to the "good wars" of recent memory, like World War II and the Cold War. But the administration understood the historic nature of its opportunity as surely as those early American politicians who created the modern U.S. Navy and passed the military budget to support it. The attacks of 9/11 served as a mobilizing opportunity—like the Barbary pirates or the

Seljuk seizure of Jerusalem in the eleventh century—for the administration to advance its foreign policy agenda of regime change, democracy promotion, military spending increases, and resource extraction. This was a crusade in deed, if not in word.

The Global War on Terror and Its Misconceptions

Fear disables rational thinking. In his book *Blink*, Malcolm Gladwell describes how rapid heartbeat and adrenaline rush distort the immediate perceptions of frightened people. They make mistakes. They see guns where there are no guns. They misread facial expressions. They come to the wrong conclusions.[25]

After September 11, the Bush administration understood the uses of fear. By keeping the country in a prolonged state of fear, the architects of the administration's anti-terrorism policy could advance a fundamentally irrational agenda. As a result, America misidentified terrorists, saw weapons of mass destruction where they didn't exist, and supported quick-draw military solutions when diplomacy would have been more appropriate. Fear disabled the rational thinking of the American electorate, which accepted the wrong conclusions of Washington policy makers.

For the Bush administration, the paranoia behind its counterterrorism campaign sustained a global crusade of unlimited scope and duration, a crusade more uncompromising even than the Cold War containment of the Soviet Union. After all, despite a climate of fear sustained by anticommunism, the United States negotiated with the Soviet bogeyman. But the Bush administration hewed to a more theological line. "We don't negotiate with evil," Vice President Dick Cheney famously remarked, "we defeat evil."[26] In such a struggle against "evil," all means can be justified, as they were during the Crusades and the Inquisition. By putting the "fear of the devil" into the American public, the Bush administration acquired carte blanche to transform not only certain U.S. policies but the entire policy-making structure.

The U.S. war on terror harkened back to the most extreme positions of the Cold War period. Washington policy hawks, including those who formulated National Security Council Report 68 and its expansion of the national security state, were never particularly satisfied with simply containing communism according to George Kennan's judicious strategy.[27] They wanted to roll back the enemy—in Eastern Europe, in Cuba, in North Korea, and China—and were ultimately dissuaded only by the nuclear and conventional military capabilities of the communist adversaries. George Bush Sr., by contrast, was a conventional cold warrior in his containment rather than rollback of Saddam Hussein in the first Gulf War. His son and many of the advisors around him had never been happy with that approach. They designed the war on terror as retaliation plus rollback—unseating the Taliban, finally getting rid of Saddam Hussein, and then proceeding to the other members of the "axis of evil" before tackling countries further down the list like Syria. This was a war that could last for generations, the administration suggested. It was a war that could take place anywhere, against anyone not "with us." In these respects, it resembled less a specific war, like the conflict in Vietnam, than the medieval Crusades and the Cold War, which both stretched across generations, took place in many far-flung locations, and targeted a very diverse group of adversaries who were not "with us."

After 9/11, the administration failed to capitalize on the international goodwill directed at Washington to broker a broad, multilateral effort against terrorism. Even Iran provided assistance for the attack on the Taliban in Afghanistan and Syria cooperated with intelligence on Islamic extremists. The Muslim Brotherhood and Hamas denounced the terrorist actions. The Council of Religious Scholars in Jordan condemned what it considered "a heinous crime."[28] Egyptian sheikh Yusuf Qaradawi and four other signatories also issued a *fatwa* demanding that the perpetrators be brought to justice.[29] The Organization of the Islamic Conference repeatedly spoke out against terrorism (which is not surprising since so many acts of terrorism have targeted Conference members).[30] At home too, virtually every Muslim organization in the United States denounced the 9/11 attacks. "American Muslims utterly condemn what are apparently vicious and cowardly acts of terrorism against innocent civilians," the statement of the Council on American-Islamic Relations read in part."[31]

The United States ignored this consensus in launching Crusade 2.0. It rejected promising overtures from longstanding adversaries, rejected the advice of previously close allies, and set dangerous precedents that will haunt U.S. foreign policy for decades. The Bush administration rationalized the use of torture and rendition. It presided over gross human rights violations at the Abu Ghraib prison in Iraq, Camp Bagram in Afghanistan, Camp Delta at Guantánamo, Cuba, in a series of rendition sites in Europe, and elsewhere. Pursuing a preventive war against Iraq and authorizing targeted assassinations, the administration broke international law.

The framing of the conflict with al-Qaeda and its supporters as a "war"—rather than a campaign for criminal justice—made certain tactical sense for the Bush administration. It wasn't possible, of course, to use a "skirmish" or a "police action" to rally the troops, launch an aggressive new foreign policy, or restrict civil liberties on a large scale.

"War," however, was precisely what al-Qaeda wanted because it meshed with Osama bin Laden's accusation that the United States and its allies were Crusaders. To declare war on al-Qaeda and cast that war in civilizational terms elevated the extremists to the level of warriors in a battle of truly biblical proportions. And the specific wars that followed—in Afghanistan, Iraq, Pakistan—served as recruitment opportunities for the extremists. The mujahideen developed a global reputation for bloodying Soviet noses in Afghanistan. They enhanced their reputation in certain circles by standing up to the modern-day Crusaders and helping to fight them to stalemate.

Al-Qaeda is megalomaniacal but ultimately marginal, even more so after bin Laden's assassination in 2011.

Compared to the Soviet adversary, al-Qaeda is minuscule. "At its peak, al-Qaeda's membership ranged between 3,000 and 4,000 fighters," writes Middle East specialist Fawaz Gerges. "There are no brigades, fighter jets, and heavy tanks in al-Qaeda's armory much less weapons of mass destruction."[32] In fact, al-Qaeda had lost its battle even before 9/11. For all the pain and suffering that the terrorist attacks caused Americans, al-Qaeda's mission wasn't focused on the United States, but rather on transforming the Muslim world. The Muslim world, however, wasn't listening. Al-Qaeda's resort to dramatic spectacle was at once a brilliant tactic and a desperate effort to boost its own fortunes. Some portion of the Muslim world did rally around al-Qaeda for a brief period, but only to protest U.S. occupation policies—first the presence of U.S. soldiers in Saudi Arabia, then in Afghanistan and Iraq—not to establish a global caliphate. According to the Pew Global Attitudes Project, Osama bin Laden's support in the Muslim world fell steadily from 2003 through 2011.[33] The use of suicide bombers to advance al-Qaeda's aims, like the last-ditch efforts of the Japanese kamikazes, only underscored the movement's marginality.

The United States and its ill-conceived response to 9/11 largely sustained al-Qaeda's reputation. Osama bin Laden wanted the United States to respond with a crusade, and the United States obliged him. A change in U.S. policy in the Middle East—fully withdrawing from Iraq and Afghanistan, supporting democracy movements in the region, accepting the role Islamists play in democratic politics, brokering a peace deal between Israel and Palestine—would deprive al-Qaeda of its mobilizing symbols.

The self-defeating problems with the war on terror were not limited to Afghanistan and Iraq. In Somalia, for instance, the administration's opposition to the Islamic Courts Union—and the support given to Ethiopian invasion of the country in 2006—helped maintain Somalia as a failed state and a more congenial place for terrorists to hide out. The CIA-led drone attacks in Pakistan, in addition to violating U.S. prohibitions against targeted assassination, served to radicalize the population in the border areas near Afghanistan. The opening of a "second front" against Muslim radicals in Southeast Asia pushed up military spending in the region without providing greater stability, particularly in the restive regions of southern Philippines and southern Thailand.

Against the backdrop of these wars and campaigns targeting predominantly Muslims, the Bush administration's effort to win "hearts and minds" was a dismal failure. It launched a 24-hour Arabic-language radio station (Radio Sawa), a 24-hour Arabic-language television station (al-Hurra), and a glossy magazine (*Hi*) targeted at teens. "Never before had America's overseas information programs been able to generate and distribute so much information so quickly to such a large audience," observes public diplomacy specialist R. S. Zaharna.[34] But speed and volume could not compete with the tone deafness of the approach. The magazine failed within two years. Despite hundreds of millions of dollars of investments, al-Hurra "is widely regarded as a flop in the Arab world, where it has struggled to attract viewers and overcome skepticism about its mission," according to the *Washington Post*.[35] Radio Sawa has done better in reaching its demographic, but only by focusing on music rather than politics.

Given the palpable effects of U.S. foreign and military policy, even a pitch-perfect campaign would have failed, just as an excellent ad campaign can't compensate for a fundamentally unpalatable product. The United States couldn't win hearts and minds because it was either deliberately or inadvertently killing too many Muslim bodies. Moreover, the permissive culture on display in these efforts—the music, the consumerism, the flaunting of traditional values—had helped radicalize an earlier generation of Muslim extremists and promised to do the same for yet another generation.[36] Many of the "soft power" tactics that had worked for the United States during the Cold War were likely to have the opposite effect on the ultra-religious.

At home as well, Bush administration policies were losing many Muslim hearts and minds as a result of the twenty-first-century versions of the Red Scares that followed both world wars of the twentieth century. With the USA PATRIOT Act, passed by Congress with near unanimity and signed into law by President Bush on October 26, 2001, the administration used national security as a trump card to dramatically expand the surveillance of U.S. citizens and the restriction of their civil liberties. But the focus was on Muslim and Arab Americans. U.S. authorities imprisoned over 5,000 foreign nationals, subjected 80,000 Arab and Muslim immigrants to fingerprinting and registration, sent 30,000 "national security letters" every year to U.S. businesses demanding information about their customers, and justified warrantless wiretapping of citizens.[37] It denied the right of habeas corpus to both American and non-American detainees and, when finally trying several detainees in military tribunals, continued to restrict their legal rights. It arrested, detained, interrogated, or deported a thousand imams and subjected mosques to surveillance and infiltration.[38]

These policies didn't produce Islamophobia. Rather, they encouraged a strong undercurrent of anti-Islamic and anti-Arab sentiment that had long been growing in the United States.

The Rise of Islamophobia

On October 11, 1985, Alex Odeh was opening the door to his office, the American-Arab Anti-Discrimination Committee (ADC) in Santa Ana, California. Odeh was a 41-year-old professor of Middle East history and Arabic, a Palestinian American Catholic, and an articulate proponent of interfaith dialogue.

Odeh had recently been in the news. He had appeared on CNN and an ABC affiliate the night before. It was the time of the hijacking of the *Achille Lauro* cruise ship by four members of the Palestine Liberation Front and their murder of disabled passenger Leon Klinghoffer. Odeh was upset about the hijacking and the murder and decided to speak out. But his televised comments condemning terrorism were edited down so that, in the end, the show aired only his praise of PLO chairman Yasser Arafat's role in defusing the hostage standoff.[39] Odeh no doubt planned to clarify his views in a scheduled talk at a local synagogue that evening. He never had the chance.

Someone had wired the door of the ADC office with a bomb. The explosion killed Odeh and injured seven others. The FBI announced that the likely perpetrator was the Jewish Defense League (JDL), an extremist organization founded in 1968. JDL leader Irv Rubin declared the allegation "absurd, obscene, and outrageous" even as the JDL itself said that Odeh "got exactly what he deserved."[40] Rubin would later be taken into custody in December 2001 for his involvement in a plot to bomb the King Fahd Mosque in Culver City and the field office of Arab-American congressman Darrell Issa (R-CA). He subsequently committed suicide in the detention facility, and the Odeh case remains officially unsolved to this day.[41]

The murder of Alex Odeh was only one example of pre-9/11 targeting of Arabs and Muslims. The year of his murder, terrorists planted a bomb at the ADC office in Boston and set fire to the Washington office. Arsonists also struck a mosque in Houston and the Washington office of the United Palestinian Appeal. Vandals targeted a mosque in Potomac, Maryland, and the Islamic Institute in Dearborn, Michigan.[42]

These were not isolated acts. A tradition of Islamophobia stretched back into the nineteenth century, when "the Muslim world was still seen as violent, fanatical, sexist, and dangerous by many Americans," according to historian Edward Curtis.[43] Two trends in the post–World War II era contributed to a spike in anti-Islamic and anti-Arab sentiment in the United States. In 1960, oil-producing countries launched the Organization of Petroleum Exporting Countries. Though created by several non-Arab countries like Venezuela, OPEC became associated in the public mind with Middle Eastern sheikhdoms like Saudi Arabia and Dubai, particularly after Arab states conducted an oil embargo during the Yom Kippur War in 1973 in retaliation for Western support of Israel.

The second trend was the birth of the Palestinian movement for self-determination. Dispossessed by the creation of the state of Israel in 1948, Palestinians ended up living in several different Arab states, which they hoped would advance their interests. When that didn't happen, however, frustrated Palestinian nationalists created al-Fatah in 1957. Much like Irish republicans in Northern Ireland and the Basque separatists in Spain, Palestinian militants seized on terrorist tactics to achieve their goal of an independent state. Other Arab groups, such as Hezbollah, also adopted terrorist tactics to strike at U.S. targets in Lebanon, such as the Marine barracks in Beirut in 1983.

Greedy Arab sheiks and ruthless Arab terrorists became the dominant stereotypes for Americans in the 1970s and 1980s. Arabs vied with Russian communists to be the default bad guys in Hollywood films. "Arabs are almost always easy targets in war movies," concludes Jack Shaheen in *Reel Bad Arabs*, his exhaustive study of stereotyped representations of Arabs.[44] The U.S. hostage situation that followed the 1979 Iranian revolution made "ayatollah" a household term of abuse and added an anti-Islamic spin to these stereotypes. "There was the '73 (Arab-Israeli) war, then the oil embargo, and suddenly we were being held responsible for things we had nothing to do with and no control over and maybe didn't even support in the first place," explained Arab American firefighter Don Unis.[45] According to polling from 1981, large percentages of Americans thought of Arabs as "barbaric," "cruel," "treacherous," "warlike," and "bloodthirsty."[46] This was a decade when the toy company responsible for Cabbage Patch dolls came out with its Nomad doll, dressed in a burnoose, described as an outcast, and pitched with the tagline: "No country will accept this heartless terrorist."[47]

These attitudes did not improve in the 1990s. The Cold War was over, the Soviet Union no more. As a result of his invasion of Kuwait and the resulting first Gulf War, Saddam Hussein was public enemy number one in Washington. The first Gulf War coincided with a major increase in hate crimes against Arab and Muslim Americans. Even during the short period between the Oklahoma City bombing and the arrest of anti-government terrorist Timothy McVeigh, during which rumors of Muslim involvement were rampant, the Council on American-Islamic Relations tabulated more than 220 incidents of hate crimes against Muslims.[48] According to an ABC poll from 1991, 59 percent of Americans associated the term "terrorists" and 56 percent associated the phrase "religious fanatics" with Arabs.[49] Throughout this time, federal authorities targeted Arabs and Muslims. The FBI used an Anti-Defamation League–paid undercover agent to spy on Arab-American organizations; the INS used secret evidence in an attempt to deport specific Arabs and Muslims.[50]

It got worse after 9/11, much worse. Suddenly it was as if every Muslim in America was wearing a target on his or her back, including those guilty of only "looking Muslim" such as turbaned Sikhs. Frank Roque, who bragged in a bar that he would "kill the ragheads responsible for September 11," shot and killed a Sikh gas station clerk.[51] "We're at war. I did what I had to do. I did it to retaliate," explained Mark Stroman, who killed two people and blinded a third. Assaults multiplied. Teenagers burned down a Sikh temple they believed was frequented by al-Qaeda supporters. In Bridgeview, Illinois, a mob of 300 bigots converged on the local mosque, shouting anti-Arab and anti-Muslim slogans. The FBI reported a surge in hate crimes from 28 in 2000 to 481 in 2001.[52] There was a rise in complaints of discrimination at work and racial profiling in airport security.[53] Immigration authorities went after Muslims and Arabs. Hundreds of detainees languished in detention centers for many months. "At least initially those held believed they could take some solace in their religion," writes journalist Stephan Salisbury. "Their prayers were greeted with hoots and derision from guards."[54]

Despite America's reputation as a haven for those seeking freedom of worship, religious intolerance has a long tradition in this country. New Yorkers mobilized to protest the city's first Catholic Church—in 1785.[55] In a pamphlet from 1854, the nativist movement singled out Catholics as people who "HATE our Republic, and are trying to overthrow it" and similarly "HATE" liberty of conscience, press, and speech.[56] The notion that Catholics were ultimately duplicitous and owed their allegiance to the Vatican, not to Washington, remained a preoccupation of Protestant American society up until the 1960 presidential elections and the eventual, but narrow, triumph of Catholic John F. Kennedy. Anti-Jewish bigotry has also been an enduring part of the U.S. tradition. Lynchings, assaults, bombings, quotas, pervasive stereotypes, Holocaust denial: anti-Jewish hate crimes and bigotry have been equally strong on the margins (in the Ku Klux Klan) and in the mainstream (the writings of Henry Ford). And with the exception of 2001, anti-Jewish hate crimes still considerably outnumber anti-Muslim incidents, according to the FBI.[57]

But today in the United States, the crusade against Muslims remains the only politically acceptable form of discrimination. Catholics have become so integrated into U.S. culture that they now represent the majority of U.S. Supreme Court justices. There are thirteen Jewish members of the Senate and 31 in the House. Despite representing a comparable percentage of the population as Jews, the Muslim community has only sent two of its members to Congress. Racist, anti-Catholic, and anti-Jewish sentiments are rarely heard in the media—and their utterance almost always triggers an uproar and often ends a career. Anti-Arab and anti-Muslim sentiments, on the other hand, often go unheralded.

In a 2004 program after the death of PLO chairman Yasser Arafat, radio host Don Imus held the following exchange with his on-air partner Sid Rosenberg.[58]

> DON IMUS, host: They're [Palestinians] eating dirt and that fat pig wife [Suha Arafat] of his is living in Paris.
> ROSENBERG: They're all brainwashed, though. That's what it is. And they're stupid to begin with, but they're brainwashed now. Stinking animals. They ought to drop the bomb right there, kill 'em all right now.

Although the remarks stirred some controversy, Imus wasn't forced to resign until three years later when he made overtly racist and sexist comments about the Rutgers women's basketball team.

In short, Islamophobia remains a powerful force in American society as much for its periodic efflorescence as for its unremarked-upon ubiquity. These sentiments explain in part why, presidential declarations notwithstanding, the American public viewed the global war on terror in crude, religious terms.

These, then, are the three unfinished wars of the West against the rest. The Crusades continue to shape how the West defines the actions of Muslims and the nature of

Islam. The Cold War contributes a framework for liberals and conservatives to fashion a new consensus around the need for a new "good fight" against a "totalitarian" enemy. And the global war on terror, which targeted Muslim majority countries and led to the death and injury of countless Muslims, has created an atmosphere of fear in which latent Islamophobia has metastasized at home and sowed the seeds of anti-Americanism abroad.

In 2008, Americans elected a new president who promised to push the reset button on U.S. relations with the international community, including the Muslim world. His supporters and critics alike were eager to find out whether President Obama would in fact end Crusade 2.0.

FOUR

The Crusade Continues

President Obama was careful to groom his non-Muslim image during his presidential run in 2008. He was repeatedly seen praying in churches, and he assiduously avoided mosques. He didn't make any campaign appearances with prominent Muslims or Arabs. He talked about his "personal relationship" with Jesus Christ. The day after he clinched the Democratic Party nomination in June, he gave a speech to the American Israel Public Affairs Committee (AIPAC) in which he reaffirmed that he was "a true friend of Israel."[1] Although he would occasionally mention his Muslim relatives and the time he spent as a child in Indonesia, Obama did whatever he could to emphasize two out of the three major monotheisms at the expense of the third.

His opponents did just the opposite. They mispronounced his last name as Osama. They emphasized his middle name, Hussein.[2] They challenged his birth records and distributed false reports that he studied in a radical madrasa as a child in Indonesia.[3] They disseminated a photo of Obama wearing a turban on a visit to Kenya to "prove" he was a Muslim.[4] They asserted that he was too close to the Palestinian cause. Controversial right-wing blogger Debbie Schlussel aggressively tried to link Obama to the Nation of Islam's Louis Farrakhan and Palestinian scholar and activist Edward Said.[5] In July 2008, after Obama appointed Mazen Asbahi as his first adviser for outreach to the Muslim community, conservatives launched a smear campaign to tie Asbahi to radical imams. The allegations were false, but Asbahi resigned quickly to avoid dragging down Obama's campaign.[6]

In September 2008, readers across the United States opened up their Sunday papers to discover a free DVD entitled *Obsession: Radical Islam's War with the West*. The movie had been made several years before. But the Clarion Fund, a pro-Israeli organization connected to John McCain's presidential campaign, decided to distribute the DVD in swing states prior to the 2008 election. The movie didn't tie the Democrats directly to radical Islam but gave the impression that politicians in the Obama mold would appease Osama bin Laden and his cohort.

The campaign against Obama had a very thirteenth-century feel to it, for it resembled the rumors spread by an earlier generation about Frederick II. As the head of the Holy Roman Empire in the thirteenth century, Frederick spoke Arabic, kept counsel with Muslim scholars, and was so taken with Saracen culture that he created a kind of Muslim city-state in the fortress town of Lucera in Italy.[7] Even when the emperor headed the Sixth Crusade, talk of his deep-seated anti-Christian motives continued. His policy of peaceful cooperation with the enemies of Christendom—by which he managed to win back Jerusalem through treaty in 1229—was simply more proof of his apostasy. Following the lead of Pope Gregory IX, apocalyptic Christians believed that the emperor was the Antichrist.

Like Frederick II, Obama has some early connections to Islam in his past, through his father's family and during the time he spent as a child in Indonesia. Although the president is as demonstrably Christian as the Holy Roman Emperor was, Obama has been unable to convince his most extreme critics of his crusader credentials even after becoming the commander in chief of U.S. forces in Afghanistan, Iraq, and other predominantly Muslim countries. Obama's stated preference for diplomacy has sealed the deal. Since entering the Oval Office, Obama has effectively become the Antichrist of the Islamophobes. Indeed, according to a Harris poll in March 2010, 24 percent of Tea Party supporters actually agreed with the statement that Obama "may be the Antichrist."[8]

Did candidate Obama, once in office, become the "appeaser in chief," as this right-wing campaign portrayed him? As president, Obama certainly broke with Bush administration policies toward the Islamic world on a few points. He pushed ahead with his plan to remove combat troops from Iraq (with some important exceptions), promised to close the Guantánamo detention facility (only to be blocked by Congress), and pressured Israeli Prime Minister Benjamin Netanyahu's government to stop expanding settlements in occupied Palestinian lands and to negotiate in good faith (though the pressure was limited). He showed some willingness to negotiate with the Taliban to end the war in Afghanistan.[9] In a highly publicized speech in Cairo in June 2009, he also reached out rhetorically to the Islamic world even as he was eliminating the name "global war on terror" from the government's vocabulary and relying instead on phrases like "a war against a far-reaching network of hatred and violence."[10]

For Islamophobes, Obama's every action indicated his latent sympathies, including his decision to give his first interview as president to al-Arabiya television, an Arab network. In his first year in office, the president did "everything in his power to curry favor with the Arab and Muslim world" at the expense of Israel, writes former AIPAC lobbyist Mitchell Bard, overlooking the enormous economic and military support Obama continued to lavish on the principal U.S. ally in the Middle East.[11] Meanwhile, the factual slurs continued. The American Family Association mounted a campaign against the president giving away tax dollars "to rebuild Muslim mosques around the world," which was really just the usual State Department outlays for historic preservation.[12] Arch-conservative Frank Gaffney, who once occupied the looniest fringes of the Reagan administration, declared in June 2009 in the *Washington Times* that there is "mounting evidence that the president (Obama) not only identifies with Muslims, but actually may still be one himself," even after the president and his supporters patiently detailed his Christian background, beliefs, and practices.[13]

The debate over the new president's sympathies obscured a much more troubling reality. Those who supported the president's policy of engaging with the Muslim world and those who accused the president of perfidy were both ignoring the fact that U.S. foreign and military policy toward the Muslim world had largely continued intact from the Bush years. Despite the rhetoric of a president clearly more at ease with diplomacy than his predecessor, Crusade 2.0 has continued well into the Obama era.

GWOT by Any Other Name

Imagine, for a moment, that you are a Muslim living in Cairo. You've heard the new U.S. president, in his June 4, 2009, speech in your city, talk about treating your religion with respect. You have heard him talk about "civilization's debt to Islam." It is a powerful speech, and at one point a voice from the audience cries out "Barack Obama, we love you!"[14] You have had high hopes that President Obama will dramatically change the way that the United States engages the world—and the Muslim world in particular—and this speech furthers your hopes.

But when you open the newspaper or watch the television news or gather for conversation at your favorite coffeehouse, a different reality confronts you.

Virtually every day there's another report of U.S. drone attacks, which have been escalating rapidly in the Pakistani borderlands.[15] The UN special representative on extrajudicial killings submitted a report in June 2010 that identified numerous technical, legal, and ethical problems with the CIA drone attacks in Pakistan. "Testimony from witnesses and victims' family members, showed that international forces were often too uninformed of local practices, or too credulous in interpreting information, to be able to arrive at a reliable understanding of a situation," Philip Alston wrote. "International forces all too often based manned airstrikes and raids that resulted in killings on faulty intelligence."[16] As a result of these findings, Alston recommended that the United States exercise greater restraint.[17] Yet the Obama administration proceeded to do just the opposite. Drone attacks more than doubled in 2010 from 2009, with most coming *after* the UN admonition.[18] It is difficult to know how many civilians have died as a result of these attacks targeting al-Qaeda and Taliban leaders. The New American Foundation estimates that one in four casualties has been civilian, with a total in the hundreds.[19]

It's not just drones. The United States orchestrated a surge in Afghanistan. U.S. Special Forces now operate in seventy-five countries, 20 percent more than during the Bush years.[20] Meanwhile, Guantánamo remains open, the United States still practices extraordinary rendition, and assassination remains an active part of Washington's toolbox.

You were no fan of Osama bin Laden or his coreligionist Anwar al-Awlaki in Yemen. Al-Qaeda's murder of civilians violated the tenets of the Qur'an, and the extremists have targeted Muslims as often as non-Muslims. But you're concerned that the targeted assassinations of these figures and others violated national sovereignty and international law. Perhaps the most uncomfortable fact is that the United States long supported Hosni Mubarak, the Egyptian president-for-life that you and all your friends opposed, and the Obama administration shifted its stance only when Mubarak was already cornered and isolated.[21]

The civilians killed in these overseas contingency operations were predominantly Muslim. The people seized and interrogated have been mostly Muslim. The Egyptians who suffered under Mubarak's repression were mostly Muslims as well. The buildings destroyed are largely Muslim-owned. If the United States or Israel attacks Iran—and the rumors have been thick in the air for almost a decade—the victims again will be primarily Muslim people.

You are angry about all the civilian casualties. You are just as angry as Americans were after 9/11 or Britons after the 7/7 bombings in London. And your anger is not just directed at a handful of individuals or a marginal, extremist group. You are angry about the official policies of the most powerful country in the world and its allies. You might very well conclude that Barack Obama's speech in June 2009 was just words. You never liked al-Qaeda, but the rhetoric of "Crusaders and imperialists" used by al-Qaeda sounds increasingly apt. Egypt was the target of several Crusades in the Middle Ages. It suffered at the hands of Ottoman, French, and British colonial policies. And now it seems to you that the United States has adopted the imperialist, crusader mantle, even if its own people are largely unaware of it.

It's no wonder, then, that the favorability rating of the United States in Egypt, which rose immediately after the Cairo speech, subsequently suffered an even greater fall. In 2009, U.S. favorability stood at 27 percent. By 2010, it had dropped to 17 percent, the lowest recorded in the Pew surveys.[22] Egyptian public opinion is not uniquely negative. In surveys in six Middle East countries before and after the Cairo speech, the Brookings Institution and Zogby International discovered that the number of respondents optimistic about the president's approach to the region suffered a dramatic drop from 51 percent to 16 percent.[23] As analyst Juan Cole argues, "hundreds of millions of Muslims suffer from America Anxiety; they believe that a superpower is seeking to undermine and destroy their religious identity and control their resources."[24]

You are a Muslim. You are upset at U.S. policies that seem to target Muslims. But your response is not a function of your religion, just as Irish Catholic anger at British occupation policies in Northern Ireland was not theological. The issue in Ireland, as it is throughout the Muslim world, has been over sovereignty and the policies of an occupying force. The U.S. wars, occupations, raids, and repeated air strikes have produced much of this disaffection and, as political scientist Robert Pape has consistently argued,[25] most of the suicide bombings and other attacks against Western troops and targets as well. This is revenge, not religion, talking—just as it was for Americans after September 11, 2001. As commentator M. Junaid Levesque-Alam has astutely pointed out, "When three planes hurtled into national icons, did anger and hatred rise in American hearts only after consultation of Biblical verses?"[26]

Nor are you upset because as President Bush said, you hate the American way of life. You, like your friends and family, have aspirations that are not very different from non-Muslims the world over. "Numerous polls that we have conducted," writes pollster Stephen Kull, "as well as others by the World Values Survey and Arab Barometer, show strong support in the Muslim world for democracy, for human rights, and for an international order based on international law and a strong United Nations."[27] Gallup polling shows strong support in the Muslim world for freedom of speech and gender equality.[28] The protests that convulsed the Muslim world in 2011, first in Tunisia, then spreading to Egypt, Yemen, and elsewhere, demonstrate the hunger many Muslims have for greater democracy and economic justice.

Crusade 2.0 is not a holy war, except perhaps in the imaginations of Christianists obsessed with the Book of Revelations. But the military campaigns of Crusade 2.0, particularly in conjunction with the surge of Islamophobia in the United States and Europe, give U.S. and allied policies the semblance of a civilizational struggle. The Obama administration's substitution of a different name for the global war on terror has not assuaged the principal targets of Crusade 2.0. Although the new team in Washington has been even more careful than its predecessor to identify Islam as a religion of peace and to reach out to the Muslim world, Muslims simply aren't buying it.

Misreading the Arab Spring

Protesters have been gathering by the thousands to demand, nonviolently, the end of dictatorships: what's not to like? But not everyone was excited by the Arab Spring that brought down dictators in Tunisia and Egypt in 2011, precipitated a civil war in Libya that eventually ousted Muammar Gaddafi, and threatened authoritarian regimes in Yemen, Bahrain, Syria, and elsewhere.

Republican presidential candidate Michele Bachmann went out of her way to blame President Obama for the Arab Spring. "You want to know why we have an Arab Spring?" she asked her audience at a fundraiser in New Hampshire. "Barack Obama has laid the table for an Arab Spring by demonstrating weakness from the United States of America."[29] Bachmann's discomfort with the Arab Spring stems from her association between strong-arm leaders and the prevention of Islamic radicalism. In an updated version of the classic Cold War rationalization, anti-jihadists argue that the United States must support dictators around the world in the fight against the larger, more existential enemy. In Bachmann's political universe, the United States should have stuck with Mubarak just as it should have supported the repressive Shah of Iran against the countrywide demonstrations in 1979—all in order to combat political Islam.

But it's not right-wing Christianists like Bachmann who have done the most to advance this thesis. "Many liberals still think the Islamists, however mild they sound today, are bent on taking over in the long run, would abandon democracy once they got into power and would use every sort of chicanery and violence to achieve their goal," writes the *Economist*. "Liberals who hate the dictatorship of Bashar Assad in Syria fear that Islamists will emerge as the chief opposition to him. And quite a few liberals still question the sincerity of the Turkish government, widely cited by Arab Islamists as a fine example of pious politicians who play by the rules of a modern democracy."[30]

According to this *jihad* liberal approach, the Islamists, like the perfidious communists during the Cold War, have only pretended at moderation in order to fool the gullible. "The moderation that these groups have exhibited in the past few decades in places such as Egypt was pragmatism born out of compulsion, not some kind of intellectual evolution," writes Ray Takeyh of the Council on Foreign Relations. "Relieved of the constraints of Arab police states, they are free to advance their illiberal, anti-Western agendas."[31] But that hasn't been the experience so far of the Muslim Brotherhood and other organizations that combine Islam and politics. They have participated quite democratically in the re-creation of Egypt and Tunisia. This willingness on the part of the Brotherhood to engage in modern politics has drawn the ire of none other than al-Qaeda, which rejects such reformist approaches.[32]

Yet al-Qaeda remains the specter that Islamophobes see whenever more than three Muslim people gather together. Consider the portrayal of the Libyan rebels. A common trope in media coverage—on the left, on the right, and even on *The Daily Show*—has been to view those fighting to oust Muammar Gaddafi as the equivalent of the *mujahideen* that fought in Afghanistan and morphed into al-Qaeda.[33] The fact that several former Afghan fighters and a former Guantánamo detainee were among the rebel fighters certainly bolstered this association. But as even the *Wall Street Journal* pointed out in April 2011, "Islamist leaders and their contingent of followers represent a relatively small minority within the rebel cause."[34] The Transitional National Council that has replaced Gaddafi's regime includes some Islamists, and the head of the council has called for Islamic law as the main source for legislation. But the constitutions of Afghanistan and Iraq also reference Islamic law, and the Islamists in Libya have by and large rejected extremism in favor of a pluralist democratic model.[35] Libyans themselves don't seem to be particularly concerned about the prospect of radical Islam hijacking their revolution.[36]

The notion that Islamism will hijack the Arab Spring draws on earlier Crusader stereotypes of the untrustworthy Saracen and Cold War assumptions about nefarious Soviet designs. Recent experience suggests that no hijacking will take place. Democracy has continued in Turkey under the Islam-influenced party; Islamic theocrats have not seized power in Indonesia. And now the Arab Spring protesters have successfully dispelled the misconceptions that democracy and Muslim countries don't go together and that Muslims are inherently violent. In fact, as journalist Amitabh Pal points out, nonviolent efforts that challenge imperial or authoritarian power have long been a feature in the world of Islam, from the Muslim pacifists who joined with Gandhi and the Sufi peacemakers who have been active around the world to the civic resistance of Kosovar Albanians against Serbia and Palestinian activists against Israeli occupation.[37]

Islamist parties are a reality in the Middle East, just as religiously motivated parties are a reality in Europe (Christian Democrats), India (the Hindu Bharatiya Janata Party), or Israel (the Shas Party). The Muslim Brotherhood and its ilk have been playing by the rules, just as these other religious parties have largely done.[38] If we support democracy, then we must acknowledge the choice of the people, even when we disagree with that choice. For its strains of homophobia and anti-Semitism, the Brotherhood wouldn't get my vote. For its fight against both religious extremism and secular authoritarianism throughout the region, however, it gets my respect. It is part of the new pluralism in the Middle East.

The Obama administration, despite Bachmann's characterization, still stands by its men in the Middle East, whether in Bahrain or Saudi Arabia, for fear of what might take their place. It continues to fear the specter of Islamism, except for those special Islamists that, as during the Cold War, proved useful in removing Arab nationalists like Gaddafi. It continues to misunderstand the nature of political life in the Middle East. In his 1985 survey of the Arab world called *The Arabs*, journalist Peter Mansfield concluded in his final chapter that "no one can tell what political and social institutions the Arab people will have developed by the end of this momentous century. All that can be said with certainty is that, however much they derive from foreign movements and ideas, they will have a specifically Arab and Islamic character."[39] Nearly thirty years later, policy makers and pundits have yet to learn that Islam is an essential part of Arab life, and that includes politics.

During the Cold War, hawks saw communism lurking behind nearly every movement for self-determination and economic justice or against authoritarian leaders. They also saw communists behind every corner in the United States as well. This fear of the enemy at home and abroad has carried over into the world of Crusade 2.0 as well.

The War on Terrorism at Home

After Obama was elected in November 2008, terrorist plots seemed to be once again hatching everywhere in the United States. Four men in Newburgh, New York, were caught in May 2009 planning to blow up two synagogues. In October 2009, the FBI shot and killed a Detroit imam it accused of plotting revolution with the aim of establishing a separate Islamic state in America. In Portland, Oregon, federal law enforcement officials arrested a Somalia-born teenager in November 2010 for plotting to bomb a Christmas tree-lighting ceremony. In Baltimore, a 21-year-old construction worker planned an attack on a military recruitment center in December 2010.

The proliferation of terrorist plots played an important role in convincing the Obama administration in February 2010 to sign a one-year extension of the USA

PATRIOT Act—even though Obama had called the law "shoddy and dangerous" in a 2003 survey when he was running for Senate and urged substantial reform of the legislation in a 2006 speech.[40] The one-year extension passed without any new limits on wiretaps, seizure of records, and surveillance, all controversial policies during the Bush administration.[41]

Yet in a number of terrorist plots, including the four mentioned above, the major accomplice was not al-Qaeda or the Taliban. It was the FBI. The Bureau has gone undercover to lure terrorists out of their lairs. This should be reassuring. But U.S. counterterrorism policy, both at home and abroad, suffers from a carrot-and-stick problem. The sticks that the Pentagon has wielded against Muslim lands have done much to encourage the proliferation of plotting on the home front, and yet Washington pretends otherwise. And the carrots the FBI offers through its undercover operations suggest entrapment.

Law enforcement officials are not thrilled by the accusation of entrapment. After the arrest of 19-year-old Mohamed Osman Mohamud, the would-be Portland bomber, Attorney General Eric Holder said that there were "a number of opportunities that the subject in this matter, the defendant in this matter, was given to retreat, to take a different path. He chose at every step to continue."[42] Juries have basically agreed with the government position. To date, the entrapment defense has not led to any acquittals. That might change, however.

According to the Supreme Court, entrapment takes

place if "the criminal design originates with the officials of the government, and they implant in the mind of an innocent person the disposition to commit the alleged offense and induce its commission in order that they may prosecute."[43] In the Portland case, there was no plot and no accomplices before the FBI decided to intervene. The Bureau had been tracking Mohamud since 2009 when it intercepted his email exchange with a suspected terrorist recruiter. From all evidence, Mohamud was unhappy with America and possibly attracted to terrorism. He was not wholly innocent. On the other hand, as a teenager, he could have been weaned of his attraction to terrorism instead of being encouraged in his worst instincts by the FBI. Meanwhile, as the FBI focused on young Mohamud, it was ignoring young Jared Loughner, whose college performance and Internet postings should have given ample warning that he was capable of violence. But no one monitored him because he didn't fit the FBI's terrorist profile, and he shot twenty people, five of whom died, and nearly assassinated Congresswoman Gabrielle Giffords (D-AZ) in January 2011.

Likewise, the Newburgh Four didn't come up with their plan to bomb synagogues and shoot down military planes. That was the suggestion of FBI informant Shahed Hussain, who traveled around to mosques in search of potential terrorists and then dangled large sums of money in front of them to join him in "jihad." When one of the four African American converts to Islam—all marginal down-and-out figures—tried to back out of the scheme because it would kill women and children, court records indicate that Hussain pressed him to continue or else put the informant's own reputation at risk.[44] Hussain even sought to stir up the anti-Jewish sentiments of his four putative colleagues by telling them "that Jews were responsible for the U.S. wars in the Middle East and for other acts of violence against Muslims."[45]

Shahed Hussain is not the only questionable FBI informant. Osama Eldawoody continued to push Matin Siraj, a young Pakistani, to move forward with a plot to blow up the Herald Square subway station in New York in 2004 even though Siraj was uncomfortable about hurting people and wanted to first get permission from his mother.[46] An unnamed informant offered Detroit imam Luqman Ameen Abdullah, whom the FBI had been tracking for three years, $5,000 to commit a violent act during the 2006 Super Bowl. Abdullah refused to be "involved in injuring innocent people for no reason."[47] The FBI continued with their sting operation in the course of which they shot the imam in the back. Like Shahed Hussain, convicted forger Craig Monteilh also went around to mosques to drum up terrorism. At the Islamic Center of Irvine, California, "Muslims were so alarmed by his talk of violent jihad that they obtained a restraining order against him," reports the *Washington Post*.[48] These informants made a lot of money at their job of reeling in potential terrorists. Their work sounds eerily similar to the bounty hunters in Afghanistan who, after the invasion in 2001, delivered to occupation authorities anyone suspected of links to al-Qaeda or the

Taliban. That tactic produced hundreds of suspects that had nothing to do with either organization.

Whether it ultimately qualifies as entrapment or not, this FBI tactic is poisoning relations with the Muslim community. "The FBI wants to treat the Muslim community as a partner while investigating us behind our backs," says a member of the Islamic Center of Irvine. "They can't have it both ways."[49] Indeed, the FBI's approach veers dangerously close to profiling the entire Muslim community as terrorism-prone when that community has been perhaps the FBI's greatest asset in identifying extremists. According to a Duke University report, "Muslim-Americans are engaged in a heightened level of self-policing against radicalization that may help to account for the infrequency of terrorist activities by Muslim-Americans."[50] But that self-policing, alongside the "community partnerships" that the FBI has encouraged, comes with a price: self-censorship and a fear of challenging U.S. policies. "The civil rights movement would have been much less successful if its only leader was Dr. Martin Luther King Jr. and there were no 'extremists' on the horizon," concludes Arun Kundnani.[51]

The U.S. government has also criminalized any provision of "material support" to a foreign terrorist group, a law that the Supreme Court upheld in summer 2010, and used the law against Muslim charities and the individuals who direct them. "Widespread intimidation of Muslim donors and the arbitrary blacklisting of charitable organizations trample on Muslims' free exercise of religion through charitable giving, create a climate of fear and distrust in law enforcement and undermine America's diplomatic efforts in Muslim countries," observes the ACLU's Jennifer Turner.[52] As legal scholar David Cole points out, the law also criminalizes the *New York Times* and the *Washington Post* when they publish op-eds by a Hamas leader because this qualifies as providing "material support" to a designated terrorist group.[53] But the FBI isn't going after the mainstream media. It's targeting the Muslim community.[54]

The rationale for this targeting is very weak. Since 9/11, there have been eleven cases of Muslim Americans, angered by U.S. policy overseas, who have actually committed terrorist acts in this country.[55] These include the Fort Hood shooter Army Major Nidal Hasan, who killed thirteen military personnel at Fort Hood, Texas, and Sulejmen Talovi, who killed five people at a shopping center in Salt Lake City in 2007. Six of these incidents resulted in the loss of life, thirty-three people altogether. To put these numbers in perspective, there have been over 150,000 murders in the United States since 9/11.[56] Given this very low number of incidents, it's rather extraordinary that so much attention has been paid to the threat of Muslim radicalization in the United States. "Like other minority groups in American history, Muslim-Americans are suspected of harboring extremists, of imperfect loyalty to the United States, of an inability to assimilate to dominant cultures— similar suspicions surrounded German-Americans during World War I, Italian-Americans during the Anarchist and Red Scares of the late nineteenth and early twentieth-century, and Japanese Americans during World War II, among other episodes," write three researchers in their study of Muslim American terrorism.[57] Their conclusion: the facts don't support a policy of profiling. And they certainly don't justify entrapment.

In the movie *Minority Report*, Tom Cruise plays a cop who has to stop crimes before they happen by relying on psychics who can see into the future. The FBI doesn't yet have access to reliable psychics. So it's doing the next best thing: forcing these future crimes to take place in the present in order to arrest the suspect. In some cases, perhaps the crime would indeed have taken place. But in other cases, the FBI has been moving dangerously into the realm of science fiction.

Attacking the Mainstream
The Obama administration, in short, has continued most of the policies of the Bush era that threaten the lives and civil liberties of Muslims at home and abroad. This continuity should ordinarily have silenced those who had previously conducted an anti-Muslim smear campaign against Obama the presidential candidate. Once in the White House, he was, after all, proving their worst fears false by pursuing key components of Crusade 2.0.

Yet the anti-Islamic attacks continued: against the president, against *sharia* law and the Qur'an, against mosques and cultural centers, against individual Muslims. This was no random convergence of disparate haters. President Clinton once spoke of a "vast right-wing conspiracy" that was out to get him, his family, and his administration in the 1990s. As later research and the revelations of turn-coats like journalist David Brock revealed, Clinton was not being paranoid about the well-funded campaign that promoted impeachment, congressional investigations, and personal attacks.[58]

A similar right-wing effort, equally well-heeled and aggressively pursued in the media, is responsible for the current Islamophobia.[59] As journalist Max Blumenthal has shown, the open season on Muslims in summer 2010 was a carefully constructed campaign that began with a campus advocacy group, the David Project, created in 2003 to counter pro-Palestinian groups at U.S. universities and funded by Aubrey Chernick, a right-wing software entrepreneur.[60] In 2004, the Project targeted a Palestinian professor at Columbia and a planned Islamic cultural center in Boston. Overcoming the mudslinging, the professor, Joseph Massad, ultimately won tenure, and the Muslim community went ahead with plans to build the cultural center in Boston.

By then, however, the anti-Islamic activists had already moved on to their next target: the Khalil Gibran International Academy (KGIA), a secular Arabic-English elementary school in Brooklyn, New York. Pamela Geller, who would later gain fame with her attacks on the "Ground Zero Mosque," concocted wild stories that the principal Debbie Almontaser "promotes an Islamist agenda, operates in an environment populated by radical Muslim organizations and individuals, holds extreme leftist political views and aims to use the KGIA as a tool of indoctrination."[61] This was nonsense. Almontaser had worked for seventeen years in the New York public school system, collaborated with the Anti-Defamation League, and had served as a consultant to PBS, Columbia University and the Interfaith Center of New York. The "Stop the Madrassah" smear campaign effectively forced the city to fire Almontaser. In March 2010, the Equal Employment Opportunity Commission ruled that New York City's Department of Education had indeed discriminated against her, but Almontaser decided not to sue the city.[62] Meanwhile, the Department of Education moved the Academy away from its original neighborhood, then cited poor enrollment as one reason for closing it down and restarting it without the Arabic focus.[63]

This network of Islamophobes chose their targets very deliberately. The Columbia professor was no radical. The Boston mosque was endorsed by the city's mayor. The principal of the Brooklyn elementary school was a leading figure in interfaith efforts. There were no links to extremism. There were only links to Islam and to progressive politics, but that was enough. To buttress his claims of extremism in the KGIA case, for example, Daniel Pipes went as far as to suggest that "learning Arabic in and of itself promotes an Islamic outlook" and "Arabic-language instruction is inevitably laden with pan-Arabist and Islamist baggage."[64] Even during the worst Cold War days, few ideologues made such claims about Russian language programs, and in fact the CIA eagerly recruited among the program graduates. Islam, however, is in a category by itself.

This preoccupation with mainstream Islam carried over to the summer of 2010, when there was a sharp spike in Islamophobia. Pamela Geller was typical in the way she went after not a radical mosque, but an Islamic center several blocks from Ground Zero proposed by a proponent of interfaith dialogue. The "duplicitous Imam," she wrote, was building a mosque with money provided by the "very same Islamic supremacists who attacked and brought down" the World Trade Center buildings (actually the cultural center received much of its money from such suspicious organizations as the Carnegie Corporation, the Henry Luce Foundation, and the Rockefeller Brothers Fund).[65] Geller was aided by key allies in the media, particularly *Fox News*, which from May 13 to August 12, according to the watchdog outfit Media Matters, gave the mike to three times as many opponents of the center than supporters.[66] It was a replay of the campaign against the Boston mosque, but the Ground Zero zip code made it a national story. A handful of right-wing activists managed to turn something uncontroversial and vitally necessary—an initiative committed to cross-cultural engagement—into something provocative, duplicitous, and sinister.

Ironically, Imam Feisal Abdul Rauf was just the kind of "good Muslim" that conservatives loved to cozy up to in order to prove that they were not Islamophobic. In his writings, the imam quotes approvingly from Supreme Court Justice Antonin Scalia and conservative literary critic Allan Bloom, lauds corporate power unfettered by state control, believes that "anti-religionism crept in as a new state religion" in the twentieth century, and condemns Hamas as a terrorist organization.[67] The Bush administration wasn't duped when it sent the imam abroad in 2007 to Morocco and the Gulf states: he was the perfect representative of its faith-based approach.[68] That such an imam and his effort to create an interfaith center embodying Bush-era values became the target of Islamophobes demonstrates just how much the struggle has been over mainstream Islam, not terrorism or extremists.

It's not just Park51 that symbolizes the integration of Islam and American values. As a two-year study by Duke's Sanford School of Public Policy and the University of North Carolina concluded, "contemporary mosques are actually a deterrent to the spread of militant Islam and terrorism" because "many mosque leaders had put significant effort into countering extremism by building youth programs, sponsoring antiviolence forums and scrutinizing teachers and texts."[69] Mosques are "premier sites of American assimilation" that encourage civic engagement by Muslims *as* Muslims, writes another scholar of the field.[70] But Islamophobes found ordinary Muslim activism in the community and in politics as suspicious as racists once considered African American engagement in the civil rights movement, the former suspecting links to Islamofascism and the latter asserting connections to communism.

Political Impact

The Center for Security Policy is the Washington policy wing of the Islamophobic network. Founder and president

Frank Gaffney, pushed out of the Pentagon for being too far to the right of President Ronald Reagan, provides the inside-the-Beltway cachet for even the nuttiest theories. He once accused the Obama administration of changing the Defense Department's logo so that it resembled a Muslim star and crescent only to back away from the charge when it turned out that it was the Bush administration that had authorized the design.[71]

In September 2010, attempting to sustain the momentum of the summer season of Islamophobia, Gaffney and the Center for Security Policy released a report entitled *Shariah: The Threat to America*. One of the team leaders on the project was William Boykin, the former lieutenant general who'd been drummed out of the U.S. military for violating the divide between church and state with his crusading rhetoric. The report begins by stating that, according to a U.S.-government sponsored study, "the Soviet Union was, pursuant to its ideology, determined to secure the defeat of the United States and its allies and the realization of the worldwide triumph of Soviet Communism." The Soviet threat was bad enough, but today "the United States faces what is, if anything, an even more insidious ideological threat: the totalitarian socio-political doctrine that Islam calls shariah."[72] Not only are they trying to take over the world by the sword, Islamists are craftily using *law* as well.

Many Americans hear the word "*sharia*" and think only of the stoning of adulterers. But *sharia* translates roughly into "rule of law" in the Muslim world. Just as the Western legal system is interpreted differently around the world—the United States has a death penalty, Europe doesn't—*sharia* looks very different in different countries. To be sure, the Taliban in Afghanistan, with their public floggings and discrimination against women, certainly gave *sharia* a bad name. But as legal scholar Noah Feldman points out, *sharia* has a distinguished history with considerable appeal to those living in lawless societies: *sharia* promises "a just legal system, one that administers the law fairly—without bias, corruption by the rich, or government interference."[73] In the early history of Islam, *sharia* emerged as a check against the autocratic impulses of the caliph. It's no surprise, then, that the new constitutions of both Iraq and Afghanistan, two countries that suffered from the arbitrary decisions of rulers for many ears, declare Islamic law as a principal source of legislation.[74] In the West, by contrast, *sharia* functions largely as a kind of alternative dispute resolution by which Muslims can address social issues such as divorce or financial disputes.

The notion that there's a "threat" of *sharia* in the United States is as ludicrous as the Cold War fantasies that communists were taking over the school system or poisoning the drinking water. In its entire 172-page report, the Center for Security Policy cites exactly one case of *sharia* law playing any role in the U.S. legal system. In 2009, a New Jersey Superior Court judge refused to grant a restraining order to a woman who testified that her Muslim husband forced her to have non-consensual sex. The judge argued that the husband's actions were consistent with his beliefs and practices. The judge made a stupid decision and the appellate court overruled him.[75] The non-Muslim judge made no reference to *sharia* nor was there any campaign by shadowy Muslim organizations to support the husband and turn the case into a precedent. One minor case with the most slender connection to *sharia* does not translate into an imminent threat.[76]

On the basis of this ludicrous "threat," Gaffney and others managed to persuade legislators in nearly two dozen states to sponsor anti-*sharia* legislation. It was not exactly an informed group of people behind these initiatives. The sponsor of an Alabama bill, for instance, couldn't define the word when asked by a local reporter. Nor could he point to any examples of *sharia* being used either in Alabama or anywhere else in the United States.[77] "The people who are saying 'no *sharia*'? It's like they're saying, 'we want no unicorns,'" says playwright and political commentator Wajahat Ali. "People get upset about the threat of unicorns. They galvanize their base. They try to amend the law. And if they're successful, they say, 'See we protected America from unicorns!' Any sane person would say, 'Yes, but there are no unicorns in America.'"[78]

In its manufacture of a "*sharia* threat," the CSP report at least distinguishes between what it deems "good" Muslims like Indonesian leader Abdurrahman Wahid and what it calls Muslim "totalitarians." Less circumspect is one of the members of the team, David Yerushalmi, the founder of another group, the Society of Americans for National Existence (SANE). This organization has proposed a law that would make Islam illegal in the United States. Any adherent to the religion would be guilty of a felony and punished with twenty years in prison. If that weren't enough, the bill would also mandate that Congress "declare the US at war with the Muslim Nation or Umma."[79] A war on Islamofascism was simply too narrow for SANE: it endorsed holy war against the entire religion.

It would be comforting to dismiss Gaffney and his team as simply colorful characters like the people who believe that 9/11 was an inside job or that NASA rigged the moon shot in some Hollywood back lot. But Gaffney still has considerable influence through the networks the right wing has constructed over the last several decades. As he told the *Washington Post*, "Members of our team have been involved in training programs for several years now, many of which have been focused on local law enforcement intelligence, homeland security, state police, National Guard units and the like."[80]

One of these "experts" that law enforcement has relied on is Walid Shoebat, who has made a name for himself as a former jihadist who subsequently converted to Christianity. Shoebat, who also believes that most Muslims intend to impose *sharia* on America, encourages local police to indulge in religious profiling, "to look at the entire pool of Muslims in a community."[81] It's remarkable that Shoebat has any credibility at all with the authorities. He is notorious for his unsubstantiated and incendiary assertions—that Obama is a Muslim, that his candidacy was supported by al-Qaeda, that Islam "is the devil."[82] Moreover, his claim of being a former terrorist has been effectively debunked by the *Jerusalem Post* and even by former fan Debbie Schlussel.[83] Yet he continues to appear on television and before law enforcement audiences as a terrorism expert.

The Obama administration's Justice Department made a commitment to address discrimination against Muslims, with Attorney General Eric Holder giving the protection of the civil rights of Muslim a "top priority."[84] And yet, the FBI, the Justice Department, and local law enforcement agencies have all held trainings that feature crude stereotypes of Muslims, as documented by Spencer Ackerman in *Wired*. "The FBI is teaching its counterterrorism agents that 'main stream' [sic] American Muslims are likely to be terrorist sympathizers; that the Prophet Mohammed was a 'cult leader'; and that the Islamic practice of giving charity is no more than a 'funding mechanism for combat,'" he writes.[85] A briefing under the Justice Department's auspices in Pennsylvania featured a PowerPoint presentation on the "civilizational jihad" that Islam had been conducting against the West from its very beginnings.[86]

These briefings rely on "experts" with credentials as dubious as Shoebat's. At one such counterterrorism training for law enforcement in Ohio, which peddled many of the aforementioned myths, the trainer fingered a local Muslim by name as connected to the homegrown terrorist network. The terrorism suspect, it turned out, was Jordanian American Omar al-Omari, a professor who ran a Muslim outreach program for the state that was so successful that the State Department sent him abroad to publicize it. Even though the local head of the Joint Terrorism Task Force came to Omari's defense, he was eventually let go from his position because of a trivial irregularity in his job application. Reports National Public Radio, "Federal officials familiar with the case say Omari was singled out because he distinguished between extremist Muslims and mainstream Muslims in his outreach and training programs."[87]

All of this organizing and media outreach has had its impact on politics. The "Ground Zero mosque" protests attracted support from major politicians such as John Boehner and Rudy Giuliani. Even moderate Democrats such as Harry Reid and Patrick Murphy urged Park51 to relocate when in fact the former World Trade Center location, like Jerusalem, was precisely the place where interfaith dialogue was needed the most. In the 2010 elections, Tea Party organizers and candidates made outlandish statements about Islam in an attempt to curry favor with their extremist base. In calling for the defeat of Muslim congressman Keith Ellison (D-MN), leader of Tea Party Nation Judson Phillips argued that "when someone adheres to an ideology that says kill people who disagree with you that is something voters should seriously consider when they vote."[88] Sharron Angle, who ran against Harry Reid in Nevada, complained about *sharia* law taking over in Dearborn, Michigan, and Frankfort, Texas: "It seems to me there is something fundamentally wrong with allowing a foreign system of law to even take hold in any municipality or government situation in our United States." Her choice of locations was curious: Frankfort doesn't exist any longer, and

Dearborn registered on Angle's radar only because police there arrested four Christian missionaries for disorderly conduct at the Dearborn Arab International Festival.[89] Angle and Phillips were not the only Islamophobes to go down to defeat. Looking at the 2010 midterm elections, journalist Stephan Salisbury concluded that "with rare exceptions, 'Islam-bashing' proved a strikingly poor campaign tactic."[90]

Yet "Islam-bashing" continued to be part of the campaigns of key Republican presidential candidates leading up to the 2012 elections. "The Republican leadership, Rudy Giuliani and others, is committed to demonizing Muslims as a campaign tactic," Middle East specialist Juan Cole told me. "It worked for them with regard to communism in the old days, and they want to see if they can get a rise out of the American public by demonizing Muslims."[91] Newt Gingrich, Michele Bachmann, and Rick Santorum have all gone on the record with anti-Islam remarks, and only Herman Cain, the former CEO of Godfather Pizza, has apologized for his earlier, Islamophobic statements.

The political attacks on Muslims have also taken place on Capitol Hill. Peter King is a Republican congressman from Long Island who once had good relations with the local Muslim community. That is, until the Islamophobia network started to whisper in his ear. On Frank Gaffney's radio show, King declared that Muslims were not cooperating with law enforcement officials to fight terrorism.[92] As the new chair of the Homeland Security Committee, he promised to hold hearings on the threat of Muslim radicals in America, disingenuously claiming these would improve relations with the Muslim community.[93] Of course, some Muslim American radicals have planned or engaged in acts of extremism. But King had a rather difficult time explaining how stigmatizing an entire community as the primary source of extremism in America, calling a range of non-experts to testify on an extraordinarily sensitive topic, and ignoring the statistic that Muslims have provided tips in 48 out of 120 terrorist cases in the United States would somehow make Muslim Americans feel all warm, fuzzy, and patriotic.[94] In any case, King had a long history of misstatements about Islam, from his assertion that radical imams controlled 80 percent of mosques in the United States to his characterization of Muslims as "an enemy living amongst us."[95] King went on to hold three hearings and, in a testament to his political influence, testified before a British parliamentary hearing on the subject, the first American congressman to have that honor.[96]

In the conspiracy theories of Islamophobes, Muslims are on the verge of taking over the country by building mosques, imposing *sharia*, and winning *halal* certifications.[97] According to Mitchell Bard, Muslims are also taking over Congress. In *The Arab Lobby*, the former AIPAC lobbyist assumes that a multitude of different actors all coordinate their actions toward a common goal: oil-rich powers, stateless Palestinians, and Arab Americans have somehow managed to hijack U.S. foreign policy "to support Middle Eastern regimes that often oppose American values and interests."[98] They've also pushed their agenda of cultural relativism in Hollywood and in the media.

In reality, these actors rarely agree with one another. Washington's support of Saudi Arabia and Egypt has nothing to do with their being Arab and everything to do with oil and geopolitics. Bard has difficulty explaining how this all-powerful lobby failed to stem the rise of anti-Islamic sentiment, create a viable Palestinian state, or disrupt the U.S.-Israel alliance. Its influence over Hollywood has resulted in only a handful of hard-fought victories, such as the replacement of Muslim villains with neo-Nazis in the movie version of Tom Clancy's *The Sum of All Fears*.

What is important here, however, is that Bard has identified as a threat not a lobby for radical Islamic interests but a diverse set of entirely mainstream Islamic organizations. In the Obama era, the focus on Islamofascism and militant Islamists from the Bush years shifted in significant ways toward an indictment of the very "good Muslims" that the neoconservatives cultivated for their "hearts and minds" campaign. As in the Crusades, the enemy is Islam as a whole.

During the First Crusade, Pope Urban II directed his call to arms to soldiers who could afford to suit up and travel to the Holy Land. Itinerant preacher Peter the Hermit heard the call and immediately set about recruiting anyone who wanted to fight the infidel. In this Peasants' Crusade, the poorly equipped and provisioned throng set out before the official crusade could even get organized. Led by the charismatic but martially deficient Peter, the crowd of 10,000 made their way to the Balkans and into Byzantine territory where the Turkish armies wiped them out.

In our era, the right-wing attacks orchestrated by the David Project, the Center for Security Policy, and Mitchell Bard are the equivalent of this Peasants' Crusade, an ugly populist attack on Islam that has accompanied the more formal military campaign conducted by professional soldiers. These populist attacks on Islam have stained America's reputation for religious tolerance and pushed the Republican Party into far right field.

Islamophobia in the United States is very serious, for it has distorted the political debate and caused considerable suffering to Muslim Americans. In Europe, the situation is more serious still. There the debate is not just about a particular mosque or piece of legislation. It's about the very nature of European identity.

FIVE

Turning European

Andrew Berwick had a few things to get off his chest. He was not happy about the rising number of Muslims living in his society. He was particularly distressed with the political agenda of his country's liberal-left parties. These grievances gradually took over his life. He worked in the customer service department of a company, then ran his own computer programming business that went bankrupt, and finally set up a farming company, but it was all to raise money to promote his views. He didn't have many friends. He didn't have a girlfriend. So he put all of his ideas into his writing. His manifesto took nine years to write, and it cost him, by his own estimate, over 300,000 Euros to produce. The result was a rather large manuscript of 1,500 pages that draws on many of the Islamophobic authors cited in this book, such as Robert Spencer and Wafa Sultan.[1]

Berwick was certainly fixated on Islam. "We have only a few decades to consolidate a sufficient level of resistance before our major cities are completely demographically overwhelmed by Muslims," he wrote in his manifesto.[2] He had quite a lot to say about the Crusades, which he deemed a "defensive campaign." But his real preoccupation was multiculturalism. He was particularly upset at politicians and others who welcomed and encouraged the growing diversity of his country. "Multiculturalism," he wrote, "is an anti-European hate ideology designed to deconstruct European cultures and traditions, European identities, European Christendom and even European nation-states. And, as such, it is an evil genocidal ideology created for the sole purpose of annihilating everything European."

Unfortunately, Berwick was not content simply to jot down his ideas. He was an activist of a sort and believed that he could change the world.

Violently.

Andrew Berwick was the nom de plume of Anders Behring Breivik, the Norwegian mass murderer who bombed downtown Oslo on July 22, 2011, killing eight people, and then went to a Labor Party youth camp dressed as a policeman and gunned down 69 young people. Breivik did not open fire on Islam or even radical Islam. He targeted what he perceived as the primary enemy of his cherished European ideal: the left. He bombed a government building to take out the ruling Labor Party and Prime Minister Jens Stoltenberg and then went after the next generation of Labor activists.

As the news of the bombing and shooting filtered out, commentators rushed to the conclusion that the culprits were Islamic radicals. Bush administration hardliner John Bolton asserted that "it sure looks like Islamic terrorism" and CNN terrorism analyst Paul Cruikshank declared

"Norway has been in Al-Qaeda's crosshairs for quite some time."[3] Even after Breivik emerged as the prime suspect, right-wing *Washington Post* columnist Jennifer Rubin was reluctant to reverse her earlier verdict of a "jihadist hydra" at work.[4] "There are many more jihadists than blond Norwegians out to kill Americans," she wrote in a follow-up to her rush to judgment, "and we should keep our eye on the systemic and far more potent threats that stem from an ideological war with the West."[5]

Breivik at one point aligned himself with the anti-immigration, law-and-order Progress Party in Norway, which had captured nearly 23 percent of the vote in 2009. Former chairman of the party Carl Hagen was notorious for his anti-Islamic statements, including the particularly ill-chosen comment a month after the Breivik killings that most terrorists were Muslim.[6] But it wasn't just psychopaths or xenophobic parties in Norway that were indulging in such rhetoric. "Phrases such as 'secret Islamification' and 'Muslim takeover' have appeared not just on obscure web pages but also on TV and radio, in articles and in the general debate," writes Norwegian author Aslak Sira Myhre. "Islamophobia has become an accepted part of our public life."[7]

Indeed, Islamophobia has become an accepted part of *European* public life. Breivik's manifesto is only the latest in a long line of European tracts that condemn Muslims and multiculturalism. In *The Rage and the Pride*, Italian journalist Oriana Fallaci composed a harsh, violent screed against Arabs, Muslims, and all manner of immigrants. Published

shortly after 9/11, the book condemns the "reverse crusade" of Muslims whether "they come with troops and
cannons or with children and boats," Muslims who "mo-
lest us with their retrograde ignorance, their retrograde
bigotry, their retrograde religion."[8] It was not a big seller
in the United States when translated into English.[9] But in
Europe, people couldn't get enough of the short, anti-Islamic tract. It sold over one million copies in Italy and was
a bestseller in France.

   It was only the beginning. Books by Bruce Bawer,
Christopher Caldwell, and Bat Ye'or were all variations on
the same theme of Muslims taking over Europe. Anders
Breivik would cite many of these works in his own manifesto, which proved to be quite an embarrassment to these
original sources. Bawer, mentioned twenty-two times in
the manifesto, refused however to acknowledge the connection between his writings and Breivik's act. All he could
muster was a lament that he might not be able to continue
to utter his anti-Islamic slurs. "In Norway, to speak nega-
tively about any aspect of the Muslim faith has always been
a touchy matter, inviting charges of 'Islamophobia' and
racism," he wrote in the *Wall Street Journal*. "It will, I fear,
be a great deal more difficult to broach these issues now
that this murderous madman has become the poster boy
for the criticism of Islam."[10] Bawer, Fallaci, and others that
traffic in ugly stereotypes pitch themselves as antidotes to
the "politically correct" treatment of Muslims.[11]

   In the aftermath of 9/11, Europe was suddenly awash
in such anti-Islamic sentiment: in books, cartoons, po-

litical platforms, and street demonstrations. Some of that sentiment has been directed within, at immigrant populations. Some has been focused on the fringes of Europe where Muslims have long lived in countries like Bulgaria, Bosnia, and Albania. And some is reserved for predominantly Muslim countries knocking on the door of the EU, namely Turkey.

Islamophobia in the United States is ugly, politically charged, and socially corrosive. But the anti-Islamic sentiment that has been long brewing in Europe is potentially more dangerous, for it recalls earlier, murderous periods of European intolerance and threatens to subvert the entire peaceful European integration project.

European Identity at a Crossroads

During its struggle with Islam, Europe found a name for itself.

Before the eighth century, Europe didn't exist, at least not in the imaginations of the residents of this far-western rump of Asia. They lived in cities or fiefdoms or tribes. They didn't understand themselves as occupying a separate continent under the banner of a cohesive identity. After Charles Martel beat back the Muslim armies at Tours in 732, chronicler Isidore Pacensis called the victors "Europenses." This neologism, writes historian David Levering Lewis, "introduced a holistic concept that transcended (definitionally, at least) the savage particularisms of his century."[12] It wouldn't be until the Crusades, however, that a distinctive European identity came into being that was the sum of its disparate parts, defined in opposition not to Islam but to the European *idea* of Islam: as a violent, expansionist, and ethically bankrupt offense to Western sensibility. At the time, ironically, Europe was several civilizational steps behind the Muslim world, for it was Islamic philosophers and doctors and mathematicians who were building on the advances of the Greco-Roman period and bringing the innovations of the great Chinese civilization westward. And yet these Europeans, with their new collective sense of themselves, somehow believed that *they* were on a civilizing crusade against the Muslims.

A civilizational enemy did wonders for the fractious Europeans during the Crusades and after. The threat of the Saracen and the Turk persuaded Europeans to look beyond their myriad differences—territorial, religious, ethnic, political—to fashion some rough semblance of unity. They pulled together to push back the Ottoman armies from the gates of Vienna on two occasions (1529 and 1683) and defeat the Ottoman navy at the Battle of Lepanto (1571). This consensus forged of adversity reigned during peace as well as war. In his *Project for Settling an Everlasting Peace in Europe*, the noted pacifist Abbé Saint-Pierre linked a peaceful European union to the fight against the Ottoman Empire. As scholar Tomaz Mastnak concludes, "A project for European union by one of Europe's greatest pacifists thus culminated in the conclusion that it was advantageous, facile, and glorious to Christian sovereigns to go to war to 'chase the Turk out of Europe and even out of Asia and Africa.'"[13] Both William Penn and Immanuel

Kant also predicated their plans of European integration on anti-Ottomanism.

During the Cold War, too, an outside threat provided the glue that could bind together a collection of nation-states that had fought each other for hundreds of years—and nearly annihilated each other in two world wars in the first half of the twentieth century.[14] This common European home, as Charles de Gaulle imagined it, stretched from the Atlantic Ocean to the Ural Mountains. In 1951, turning their backs definitively on their traditional rivalry, France and Germany began to prepare the foundation for this European home by signing the Treaty of Paris—along with Italy and the Benelux countries—to create a common market for coal and steel. This European Coal and Steel Community became the basis for the later European Union and, in alliance with the United States, a political and economic bulwark against communism.

After the end of the Cold War, this trans-Atlantic tie began to fray. "When the ideological positions that had hitched Western Europe and the United States together during the cold war became redundant after 1989," writes scholar Ian Buruma, "people began to sense a growing rift between the two continents, as though a schism had occurred in Western civilization."[15] Europe was focusing on multilateral cooperation, first to consolidate and then to expand the EU but also as part of an emerging foreign policy predicated on cooperation and international norms. The United States, after a brief flirtation with multilateralism, shifted more toward preserving its global dominance in the economic and military spheres.[16] The alliance couldn't agree about what to do to prevent Yugoslavia from unraveling, whether to support military interventions in Rwanda and Somalia, and how to construct viable international institutions such as the International Criminal Court and implement international agreements like the Kyoto Protocol. Europe was uncomfortable with U.S. unilateralism; the United States viewed the EU and many of its member states as, at best, ambivalent partners in creating a new post–Cold War order with the United States on top.

The war in Bosnia was a defining moment in this regard, since Europe's much-vaunted commitment to human rights and prevention of genocide amounted to very little when it came to atrocities unfolding in its own backyard, particularly against Muslims. "Bosnia had a tremendous impact on Muslims in Europe," recalls Massoud Shadjareh of the Islamic Human Rights Centre in London. "Here was a culturally Muslim community that was not a very practicing community. It was very European in appearance. And then comes ethnic cleansing and onslaught, and there was no response from the rest of Europe to stop it. As Bill Clinton wrote in his book, the United States held back because Europe didn't want a Muslim state. The fact that 'never again' could happen again had a tremendous impact on the Muslim community."[17] This failure to respond would haunt European foreign policy and contribute to a greater willingness in the future to follow the U.S. military lead.

The attacks of 9/11 provided European governments with just such an opportunity to respond to aggression.

British prime minister Tony Blair, who vigorously supported NATO air strikes during the Kosovo War in 1999, became the Bush administration's chief European partner in the emerging global war on terror. But 9/11, though it seemed to draw the transatlantic alliance closer together, in fact illuminated the widening gap. Even in the most widely cited statement of sympathy—from Jean-Marie Colombani's "We Are All Americans" article in *Le Monde* on September 12, 2001—there was a note of criticism. "America, in the solitude of its power, in its status as the sole superpower, now in the absence of a Soviet countermodel, has ceased to draw other nations to itself," Colombani wrote. "Or more precisely, in certain parts of the globe, it seems to draw nothing but hate."[18] This criticism of U.S. global narcissism became a leitmotif in European reactions as the United States began to expand its war on terror beyond the initial invasion of Afghanistan. Later, several states and many ordinary Europeans would openly revolt against the Bush administration's preparations for war in Iraq and its attendant assaults on international law. Some of the largest demonstrations on February 13, 2003, against the impending invasion of Iraq—the largest mass protest in human history, involving between six and ten million people—took place in Europe: half a million in France, half a million in Germany, over 600,000 in Italy, as many as two million in Spain.[19] The Bush administration dismissed the concerns of governments and protestors alike as the fusty preoccupations of "Old Europe," in Donald Rumsfeld's famous phrase.

There were indeed other European points of view. Many Europeans cheered on the U.S. juggernaut, feeling greater sympathy for the Bush team than their own, more conflicted leaders. "The military defense against Islamic terrorism is being led today by the United States, which is playing a very similar role . . . to that role played centuries ago by Poland, when it was the rampart of Christianity," proclaimed Bishop Tadeusz Ploski of Poland. He went on to urge his fellow Christians to prevent Europe from becoming "Euro-Arabia."[20] Poland and the other countries of "New Europe" were on the whole more sympathetic to the Bush administration's policies toward the Islamic world, and they often made reference to their role in battling the Ottoman Empire—at the gates of Vienna in the case of Poland or during centuries of struggle in the Balkans.

In the end, only British troops and a handful of Polish soldiers joined with the Americans in the invasion of Iraq, with Denmark providing some naval forces. Other European countries deployed a few troops after the initial invasion to maintain order. Some countries refused even this minimal endorsement. France took a steadfast antiwar position; Turkey refused to allow the United States to use its military bases to stage the invasion. But even the qualified support for the war by European ruling parties, like Spain's Popular Party, made them vulnerable at the polls and untrustworthy in the eyes of the Muslim world. "Europe's involvement in the war in Iraq," writes Turkish novelist Orhan Pamuk, "caused the keenest disappointment in non-western countries and, in Turkey, real anger."[21]

In its contribution to Crusade 2.0, the United States orchestrated attacks on Kabul, Baghdad, and, later, Tripoli. The Bush administration argued that it was fighting the enemy "over there" so as not fight them on American streets. European Islamophobes believed that they were already fighting the war at home. Muslims will conquer "Europe's cities, street by street," the *Weekly Standard*'s Christopher Caldwell predicted.[22] Europe has evolved, according to Israeli polemicist Bat Ye'or in her book *Eurabia*, "from a Judeo-Christian civilization, with important post-Enlightenment secular elements, into a post-Judeo-Christian civilization that is subservient to the ideology of *jihad* and the Islamic powers that propagate it."[23] These Islamophobes detected a malaise in Europe comparable to the failure to stand up to Nazism in the 1930s or communism in the 1940s. And naïve European multiculturalists were not just watching the barbarians enter the gate, they were actively ushering them in.

Changing Demography

European nationalism, like gaslights and bowlers, became passé during the Cold War. At the global level, an international architecture governing law, trade, and development gradually expanded its jurisdiction, and Europeans by and large supported this globalization. Some Basques, Corsicans, and Macedonians held out hope for separate states, but secession was next to impossible in those years. In fact, slowly but surely, Europeans were going in the opposite direction of deeper integration. They were even contemplating, near the very end of the Cold War, giving up such potent national symbols as their currencies. Thinkers as varied as business analyst Kenichi Ohmae and former French diplomat Jean-Marie Guéhenno rushed to inscribe the epitaph for the nation-state,[24] and it was not uncommon in academia to speak of nationalism, as E. J. Hobsbawm wrote in 1990, as "no longer a major vector of historical development."[25]

Such judgments were, to say the least, premature. Nationalism, which had neither disappeared nor even really hibernated during the Cold War, exploded in a Europe fast approaching the millennium.[26] Nationalist movements played critical roles in the 1989 revolutions in Eastern Europe, the disintegration of Yugoslavia beginning in 1991, the break-up of Czechoslovakia in 1993, and the dissolution of the Soviet Union over that same period. It wasn't just Europe east. The Scots established their own parliament, the Flemish and the Walloons came close on several occasions to a formal Belgian divorce, and France experienced a revival of Breton, Provencal, and Alsatian culture and identity. These nationalist movements organized against empires, federations, and states, structures in other words that they perceived as suppressing popular demands for self-determination and self-expression.

But there was another target of nationalist energies: minorities and immigrants, many of them Muslim.

Muslims had lived for a long time in the former Ottoman lands of Albania, Bulgaria, and much of Yugoslavia. Beginning in the 1950s, however, many Muslims from

Turkey and Yugoslavia traveled westward to become guest workers to do the dirty, dangerous, and difficult jobs that Swiss and Germans and Swedes increasingly didn't want to do. Other Muslim immigrants sought opportunities in their former colonial metropoles: North Africans in Paris, South Asians in London, Indonesians in Amsterdam. By the 1970s, this initial wave of guest workers, students, and asylum seekers was augmented by the migration of their family members.[27] In the 1990s, the removal of internal borders in an expanded Europe increased the flow of migration, mainly from countries to the east like Poland and Romania.[28] Muslims from the Balkans sought refuge in western Europe during the wars in former Yugoslavia, and Albanians and Turks continue to rank high among non-EU nationals coming to the EU.[29] European countries were becoming more multicultural even as they stubbornly clung to their old-fashioned notions of unitary cultures and continued to accord second-class status to the foreign-born at the workplace and in the public sphere. Europeans endlessly debated this multiculturalism. But as the Swiss-born Tariq Ramadan has observed, "Multicultural society is a fact, there is no being for or against it."[30]

Still, there has been a great deal of pushback. As early as the 1960s, conservative and far-right parties began to express their concerns about the potential challenge that immigration posed to their concept of national unity. British Conservative Party politician Enoch Powell, in his infamous "Rivers of Blood" speech of 1968, looked in horror at the rising number of Commonwealth faces in the British crowd and predicted bloody confrontation arising from "a dangerous fragmentation within society."[31] Much later, in October 1985, a special edition of the French newspaper *Le Figaro* asked, "Will we be French in thirty years?"[32] The fear of losing British-ness or French-ness would become a central concern for those not only fearful of a rising tide of immigration from below but also homogenization imposed from above by European integration (as well as globalization and Americanization). A demographic deficit compounded these fears. With European birthrates far below replacement level—even in Catholic countries like Italy and Spain—many Europeans looked into the mirror of the future and saw only the multicultural image of America. And increasingly this image of multiculturalism had a Muslim cast. Compared to the United States, where Muslims account for less than one percent of the population, European Muslims constituted a much larger share: 5.7 percent in the Netherlands, 6 percent in France, and 5 percent in Germany.[33]

In the immediate post–Cold War period, the face of European racism was Jean-Marie Le Pen. This unabashed xenophobe, famous for his anti-Jewish and anti-immigrant remarks, struck such fear into the hearts of the French majority that his surprising second-place finish in the 2002 elections brought more than a million protesters into the street on May 1 (and an 80 percent turnout in the run-off four days later to reelect President Jacques Chirac).[34] Other parties and figures, such as Jorg Haider in Austria and the Vlaams Blok in Belgium, clawed their way into headlines and parliaments. Their platforms showed many similarities: anxiety over the impact of immigration on national culture, skepticism about the European Union and its institutions, and an emphasis on law and order. But for all the media attention they attracted, they didn't yet have much impact on European policies.

In the 1990s, the debate around immigration focused on race and ethnicity. But after 9/11—and the subsequent terrorist attacks in London and Madrid—the religion of immigrants suddenly became of prime importance to both state and society. Because several attackers had been affiliated with particular mosques—the 9/11 hijackers with the Taiba mosque in Hamburg, Richard Reid the "shoe bomber" with the Brixton mosque in London—state security services began to pay much greater attention to Islamic institutions. The German authorities raided mosques; the British authorities interrogated imams; the Dutch monitored Friday prayers. Suspects were rounded up, but most of them turned out to have nothing to do with terrorism. The Spanish arrested sixteen North Africans on suspicion that they were concocting chemical weapons with the compound ricin, but it turned out that the suspected bottles contained nothing but cologne, olive oil, honey, ammonia, and washing powder.[35] The Italian authorities arrested twenty-eight Pakistani street vendors whose "fanatical texts" turned out to be nothing more than quotations from the Qur'an.[36] Some plots were indeed disrupted—such as the 2006 airline bombing plot that involved several British-born Muslims—but Muslims in Europe couldn't help but feel unfairly targeted because of the criminal acts of a few and the imagined plots of a few more.

In Britain, reports Arzu Merali of the Islamic Human Rights Centre in London, respondents to her organization's surveys reported high incidents of anti-Islamic sentiment even before 9/11: 35 percent of respondents reported experiencing Islamophobia in 1999 and 45 percent in 2000. "We did a more sophisticated survey in 2004 and Islamophobia went up to 80 percent," she says. "That was a disaster. And nothing has really gotten better since then."[37]

The anti-Muslim sentiment reinforced the anti-immigrant sentiment. Now that many European economies were stagnant and surplus workers could be gotten from the new EU member states, the communities that once built the subways and bridges and office buildings of a bustling Europe had become little more than a despised underclass. They suffered from discrimination in employment, education, and social services. But Islamophobes paid no attention to the legacies of racism. Immigrants, sniffed Christopher Caldwell, "bring a lot of disorder, penury, and crime."[38] Worse, they were sponging off the state. A TV ad for the far-right Swedish Democratic Party in the 2010 elections, for instance, showed a white pensioner losing out in a race for her benefits to a crowd of burqa-wearing mothers.[39] The European right was dusting off many of the characterizations used to disparage African Americans, that they were "welfare queens" and suffered from various "pathologies" related to being an "underclass." Each far-right party added its own flourishes. The Northern League in Italy, for instance, distributed bars of soap to voters in the March 2010 elections for people to use "after touching an immigrant."[40]

As with apologists for U.S. racism of a previous era, European Islamophobes rarely reflected on whether legitimate grievances rather than, in the xenophobic imagination, allegiance to a dangerous religious ideology preoccupied Muslims on the continent. As writer Pankaj Mishra points out, "It is more likely that the majority of European Muslims worry more about unemployment, discrimination, and inequality than about setting up an Islamic caliphate."[41] Overt racists talk of genetics; the modern Islamophobe prefers to talk about culture. "Some have said I argue that the achievements of immigrants from Muslim countries are lower because of genetic reasons; this is quite wrong," argues Thilo Sarrazin, the prominent German Social Democrat who made headlines by arguing that Muslim immigrants will be the death of his country. "It has to be a matter of culture, and Islam is that culture."[42] And just as racist ideology connected the "pathologies" of African Americans to the overall backwardness of Africa, so too did the Islamophobes tie the deficiencies of Muslim immigrants to what Caldwell calls the "penury, servitude, violence, and mediocrity of Muslim societies worldwide."[43]

By fall 2010, what had once been consigned to the fringes of European opinion had moved to the very center of the political debate, even in countries with reputations for tolerance. In Sweden, for instance, the far-right Sweden Democrats dislodged the ruling center-right coalition in September elections by winning 5.7 percent of the vote and gaining their first seats in parliament. In the Netherlands, anti-Muslim populist Geert Wilders helped form a new government. In Denmark, Norway, Austria, and Italy, the far right acquired significant parliamentary power.[44] In the new EU countries of eastern Europe, anti-Islamic sentiment flourished even in the absence of Muslims. In the Czech Republic, where the Muslim population is somewhere around .1 percent, an anti-mosque organization vowed to "fight against the Islamization of the Czech Republic," and a former prime minister declared that Islam was "an anti-civilization spreading from North Africa to Indonesia" that was "financed partly from oil sales and partly from drug sales."[45] In Poland, with a similarly minuscule Muslim population, an improbable alliance of skinheads and Buddhists organized an anti-mosque protest.[46] In Bulgaria, the far-right party Ataka lived up to its name by attacking Muslim worshippers at the mosque in Sofia.[47]

Before 9/11, racists and xenophobes made noise largely on the margins. Now they made laws in the parliament. In this regard, the Swiss referendum banning minaret construction, which passed in November 2009, attracted perhaps the greatest attention worldwide. After all, Switzerland is itself a model of ethnic and linguistic cohabitation among French, German, Italian, and Romansch-speaking communities. Roughly 350,000 Muslims live in the country, approximately 4.3 percent of the population, and rely on about 200 mosques and prayer spaces. There are, however, only three minarets in all of Switzerland. As justice minister in a right-wing government, billionaire industrialist and hard-right politician Christoph Blocher first tried to use zoning laws to push through a minaret ban but was unsuccessful. Two right-wing parties then attempted to push the ban through the Swiss parliament and failed. The far right turned to the referendum process only to run up against the opposition of the government, the Catholic and Protestant churches, the business community, and cosmopolitan voters. Yet, on November 29, 2009, the referendum passed with 57 percent of the vote. The fear factor played a major role, as pro-referendum activists employed the most violent stereotypes of Muslims.[48] It was a tactic that played well across Europe. Although European editorial writers blasted the Swiss results, the decision turned out to be rather popular among citizens of France, Spain, Germany and elsewhere.[49]

Also popular have been campaigns against headscarves. These head coverings that some Muslim women wear range from a simple scarf to a full-length *burqa* that leaves only a small mesh screen for the eyes. With the strict separation of church and state of its *laicite* policy, France has pioneered laws against Muslim headscarves. In 2004, the country passed a bill banning headscarves from French schools—along with other obvious religious symbols including the Star of David and the cross. In 2010, the French parliament approved a ban on full-face veils, worn by fewer than 2,000 women in a Muslim population of five million.[50] Amnesty International condemned the ruling as an abridgement of freedom of expression; Tariq Ramadan wisely pointed out that "compelling a woman to wear a hardscarf is against Islam, and compelling her to remove it is against human rights."[51] Yet other European countries— and regional authorities within countries—have instituted or are considering bans on the *burqa* or other forms of Muslim headscarves.

Behind these laws on minarets and *burqas* lies a belief that Muslims will somehow take over Europe, through immigration or sheer production of children. European countries have tightened their immigration laws and implemented baby-friendly laws to encourage reproduction by natives. The fears of fertility rate declines are very real: the only European country that produces children above the replacement rate of 2.1 children is Turkey (and many Europeans wouldn't even include Turkey in their club). Most European countries are clustered near the bottom: Czech Republic (1.25), Romania (1.27), Poland (1.29), Italy (1.32).[52] But the fear of Muslims taking over is a myth. The most recent Pew Research study projected the Muslim share of European population to rise a mere 2 percent by 2030.[53]

Islamophobes would be hard-pressed, in any case, to define which Muslims they expected to take over, given the tremendous diversity of the community and the considerable religious, ethnic, and political cleavages within it. Moreover, they might discover in the event that Muslims "took power" that not much would change. As researcher Jytte Klausen points out, "European Muslims are overwhelmingly hostile to extremism, support democratic processes, accept the duties of citizenship, and are evolving distinctively local styles of Muslim identities."[54]

The targets of European Islamophobia, as in the United States, have been the very mainstream of the religion, not the extremists. Islamophobes have gone after Mohammed, the minaret, and the headscarf. These Crusaders have complained about ordinary Muslim immigrants having babies, not plotting violent acts. They have expressed fear of increased participation by Muslims in democratic politics, linking that not to the U.S. civil rights movement but to Jerry Falwell and Christian fundamentalists.[55] Geert Wilders, the Dutch politician who leads the country's third largest party, has called the Qur'an a "fascist book" that should be banned.[56]

And it's not just the right wing any longer. "What makes anti-Muslim racism so lethal is that unlike populisms of the past, Islamophobia has broad appeal across the political spectrum, from the far left to the far right and irrespective of class or educational level," writes journalist Paul Hockenos.[57] In France, the *burqa* ban received a total of two "no" votes in the two houses of the French parliament. More than 50 percent of Germans and Spaniards "rate Muslims unfavorably," according to a Pew Global Attitudes Project poll from 2008.[58] Europe also has its share of *jihad* liberals, like Martin Amis and Regis Debray, who give Islamophobia the veneer of a political consensus. These *jihad* liberals, like their American counterparts, are not just concerned about Muslims. They're also exercised by the policies of tolerance that they believe have deliberately or inadvertently encouraged radical Islam.

Target: Multiculturalism

Just as the Cold War was coming to an end, conservative critics in America such as Allan Bloom and William Bennett began to attack a philosophy they felt was undermining Western values. Multiculturalism, which celebrates ethnic and cultural diversity, had become mainstream in education, the corporate sector, government contracting, and the entertainment world. More women and minorities were suddenly visible in boardrooms, Hollywood movies, and college syllabi. These changes were driven in part by social movements and in part by consumer preferences. Either way, the critics were upset at what they perceived as a challenge to dominant culture and the politics of assimilation, and they lamented what Arthur Schlesinger called "the disuniting of America."[59]

After 9/11, these critics began to reformulate their critique of multiculturalism to incorporate anti-Islamic sentiment. Multiculturalists committed the cardinal sin of "cultural relativism" that put all cultures on an equal footing. This, as academic Bassam Tibi and others wrote, was the Achilles' heel of Western civilization, the vulnerable spot where the Islamic sword could strike.[60] Whereas cultural chauvinists would bar the door to Islam, multiculturalists would swing it wide open, and even the most anti-Western forces could enter. For this reason, Samuel Huntington labels multiculturalism "basically an anti-

Western ideology."[61] For the Somali-born former Dutch parliamentarian Ayaan Hirsi Ali, multiculturalism has prevented teachers in the West "from openly challenging the beliefs of Muslims children and their parents."[62] For the team behind the CSP report on the "threat of *sharia*," multiculturalism has produced a "cultural anemia" in the United States, while right-wing pundit Dinesh D'Souza goes so far as to claim that multiculturalism led directly to 9/11.[63] That's a lot to pin on a philosophy that's far from radical, that's grounded in democratic practice and universal values, and that's been widely adopted by corporations and universities. The feeble attempts to caricature multiculturalism merely exposed the frustrations of social conservatives incapable of beating back the demands of politically energized minorities.

The attack on multiculturalism in Europe reflected a similar anxiety over the transformation of putatively homogenous societies. Conservatives were obsessed with the left and the liberal culture that had made a present virtue of multiculturalism out of the past necessity of guest workers. The Netherlands, for instance, once prided itself on its tolerance of hash cafes, prostitution, and the increasingly diverse nature of its population. In the 1990s, however, a "new realism" descended upon the country as politicians in the post–Cold War climate began to question liberal Dutch assumptions, particularly related to immigration.[64] These politicians addressed what Richard Nixon used to call the "silent majority," the presumed bourgeois bedrock of the society, with what would previously have been considered shocking directness. Islam is a "hostile" and "backwards" culture, argued Pim Fortuyn, one of the key figures in this European backlash against multiculturalism. The flamboyantly gay Fortuyn, whose rise to prominence owed much to Dutch traditions of tolerance, nevertheless managed to inject his views into the very mainstream of Dutch society, prior to his assassination by an animal rights activist in 2002.

The Dutch swerve toward intolerance mirrored a much larger trend in Europe. Multiculturalism, and its presumed connection to the left, was under attack throughout the continent for its alleged encouragement of minorities to hold onto their identities. The *jihad* liberals of Europe too took issue with this identity politics. They opposed multiculturalism "not from the conservative point of view, that people have to assimilate into some old-fashioned kind of society," observes analyst Arun Kundnani, but rather because "multiculturalism is against Enlightenment values."[65] Whether it was the presumably universal values of the Enlightenment tradition or the parochial culture of an imagined homogenous society, the critique boiled down to a simple demand: immigrants had to assimilate or leave.

European countries were experiencing an upheaval similar to the United States during the civil rights era. Muslim citizens were becoming politically engaged, demanding equal rights. Europeans had to redesign political and social structures to meet the needs of newly politicized minorities, and a sizable portion of the population simply didn't want to do so (just as much of the American South and a dispiriting number of liberals viewed the civil rights movement at the time as merely disruptive).[66] Rather than rise to the challenge of multiculturalism, many European politicians simply threw up their hands. Chancellor Angela Merkel, for instance, declared that multiculturalism in Germany was a failure and that it was an illusion to think that Germans and foreign workers could "live happily side by side." British prime minister David Cameron urged European governments to practice "a lot less of the passive tolerance of recent years and much more active, muscular liberalism."[67] The attack on multiculturalism by the right only encouraged more of what they disliked in the first place. "This intolerance of cultural difference and demand for total assimilation led to a converse reaction: the embrace of Islam, partly as a form of rebellion against an inhospitable social environment," writes Peter Mandaville, a specialist in political Islam.[68]

The nationalist extremists who have led the fight against multiculturalism might be parochial in perspective, but they are transnational in tactics. Many of the leaders of the anti-Muslim parties in Europe gathered in Jerusalem in December 2010. There was René Stadtkewitz of the Freedom Party, a new German split off from the Christian Democratic Union, Heinz-Christian Strache, the chairman of the Freedom Party of Austria, Belgian politician Filip Dewinter of the Flemish nationalist Vlaams Belang Party, and Kent Ekeroth of the national and anti-Islamic Sweden Democrats. They met with Jewish settlers in the West Bank, received a congratulatory note from Sarah Palin, and released a Jerusalem Declaration that decried the "new, worldwide totalitarian threat: fundamentalist Islam."[69]

Links to U.S. extremists have also expanded. The English Defence League, a recent far-right group that has grown out of soccer hooliganism, has hooked up with the Tea Party movement's Rabbi Nachum Shifren and leading Islamophobe Pamela Geller to inject anti-Islamic sentiment into the mainstream political debate in their respective countries.[70] Atlanticists once used a shared anticommunism to underscore the importance of the transatlantic relationship. A new generation was using Islamophobia. "We cannot afford to lose Europe," writes Tony Blankley of the hard-right *Washington Times*. "We cannot afford to see Europe transformed into a launching pad for Islamist jihad."[71]

These right-wing groups have been concerned with the threat from far away in Pakistan and the threat within their own societies. But they express some of their greatest angst about the threat on the borders of Europe, which recalls the Ottoman assaults on Vienna and the earlier challenges of the Crusader era. Even today, more than a decade after the end of the Yugoslav wars, the peddlers of Islamophobia write about the coming caliphate in the Balkans.[72] Most of this is warmed-over Serbian chauvinism about Muslim massacres, mercenaries, mothers, and mosques funded by the Saudis. The region is far from stable or peaceful, given Bosnia's fractiousness, Serb-Kosovo disagreements, and Greek refusal to grant Macedonia the right to use its name. But religion, and radical Islam in particular, play little role in this drama.

A little further south, however, lies a much greater preoccupation for those involved in Europe's anti-Islamic campaigns. In the eleventh century, the Seljuk Turks changed the balance of power in the Middle East, which precipitated the Crusades. A thousand years later, the Turks are once again disrupting the status quo in the region, this time nonviolently. And the advocates of Crusade 2.0 are ready.

The Challenge of Turkey

After World War I, the father of modern Turkey, Kemal Ataturk, created a new country out of the unpromising materials left behind by the collapsed Ottoman Empire. The modernizing military officer from Salonika patterned his new secular state on the French model: strong central power, a modern army, and a strict relegation of Islam to the private sphere. This was no easy process. The government banned Islamic political parties and discouraged the wearing of headscarves. Ethnic and religious minorities suffered from a Turkification campaign. And in 1924, Ataturk formally ended the Islamic caliphate, a rather dusty institution headquartered in Istanbul.

That decision in 1924 continues to haunt the relationship between Islam and the West. Al-Qaeda has launched its terrorist attacks in part to reverse Ataturk's action. For those critical of Islam, on the other hand, Ataturk's bold move remains a model for the whole Muslim world that Turkey should have more vigorously exported.[73]

Neither option, however, is particularly appealing today. Restoring the caliphate is as much a preoccupation among most Muslims as retaking Jerusalem is for most Christians. As for Kemalism, several countries indeed attempted to impose the Turkish solution on their populations: the shah in Iran, the Baathists in Syria, Gamal Abdel Nasser in Egypt. But Islam didn't go gently into the private sphere. "One of Kemalism's legacies is pent-up rage among the lower classes, to whom so few of the economic benefits flowed, and who greatly resented the assault on Islam," writes Vali Nasr.[74] That anger has greatly encouraged the growth of political Islam throughout the Muslim world.

Turks, too, have also had second thoughts about the Kemalist model and its entrenched militarism, forced ethnic homogenization, and increasingly ineffectual economic policies. Those second thoughts have led to a rehaul of the Turkish system and a rethink of Turkey's place in the world. Ataturk remains an extraordinarily popular figure in Turkey, but the pictures of him fingering prayer beads on sale in the shops of Istanbul suggest an ongoing reevaluation of his legacy. The Turkish model today combines Islam with democracy, market reforms, and creative diplomacy, which is not exactly what Ataturk had in mind.

In 2002, the Islam-influenced Justice and Development Party came to power and then enlarged its political base after the 2007 and 2011 elections. Guided by Foreign Minister Ahmet Davutoglu, a former academic who provided a blueprint for the country's new diplomacy in his 2001 book *Strategic Depth*, Turkey pledged "zero problems with neighbors." In foreign policy terminology, Davutoglu proposed the carving out of a Turkish sphere of influence via canny balance-of-power politics. Like China, it has promised not to interfere in the domestic affairs of its partners. It also made a major effort to repair relations with those near at hand—Iraqi Kurdistan, Armenia, Cyprus, Greece, Syria—and struck up new friendships with those further away in Russia, Africa, and Latin America.

A friend to all sides, Turkey is offering its services as a diplomatic intermediary, even in places where it was persona non grata not long ago. "Not many people would imagine that the Serbians would ask for the mediation of Turkey between different Bosniak groups in the Sandjak region of Serbia," observes Sule Kut, a Balkans expert at Bilge University in Istanbul. "Turks were the bad guys in Serbian history. So what is happening? Turkey has established itself as a credible and powerful player in the region."[75]

Turkey is aspiring to a global role. It is remaking the politics of the Middle East and challenging Washington's traditional notion of itself as the mediator of last resort in the region. Teaming up with Brazil, Turkey fashioned a compromise to head off confrontation with Iran over its nuclear program (which the Obama administration managed to shoot down).[76] Along with Spain, it initiated the Alliance of Civilizations, a UN effort to bridge the divide between Islam and the West. It also tried to work its magic in negotiating an end to the blockade of Gaza, removing obstacles to the withdrawal of U.S. forces from Iraq, resolving the brouhaha around the cartoon depiction of Mohammed, and hosting UN meetings on Somalia. At the level of the global Muslim community, a Turk, Ekmeleddin Ihsanoglu, now heads up the 57-member Organization of the Islamic Conference, the leading international voice of Islamic states.

The Turkish model of transitioning out of authoritarian rule while focusing on economic growth and conservative social values has considerable appeal for developing countries, particularly in the Muslim world and particularly for states transformed by the Arab Spring. Here's a predominantly Muslim country that has become more democratic even as it raises its religious profile. Egypt under Gamal Nasser was once the pole star of Arab nationalism; Saudi Arabia became the exporter of conservative Wahhabism; Iran established itself as the center of the Shi'a revival. And now Turkey has put itself forward as this year's model. Even the United States can't resist falling in behind the market leader. Washington is working closely with Ankara to prepare for a post-Assad future in Syria.[77] After joining the calls for Bashar al-Assad to step down, Turkey has been opening its borders to Syrian refugees and dissidents. Whether funding the Libyan rebels or providing early support for the Egyptian protesters or reaching out to Somalia or attempting to prepare Syria for a soft landing, Turkey has become an indispensible power.

Ankara's attempt to transcend zero-sum thinking was not an easy task during the "with us or against us" years of the Bush administration. In addition, periodic tensions have arisen around U.S. congressional resolutions on the

Armenian genocide, still a touchy issue in Turkey. Washington has not been happy with some of Turkey's friends, like Iran or Hamas. As a result, Turkey has had to finesse its relationship with the United States in order to remain a key NATO ally *and* a challenger to American power in the region.

Perhaps the chief irritant has become Turkish relations with Israel. In the Gaza flotilla incident of May 2010, for instance, the Israeli military forcibly boarded the *Mavi Marmara*, which was carrying humanitarian aid to Gaza, and killed nine passengers, all of them Turkish. Although Turkey is a member of NATO, the United States focused its wrath on Turkey, not Israel. The U.S. Congress was nearly unanimous in its support of Israel, which "invoked its right to self-defense," according to Rep. Steny Hoyer (D-MD).[78] The Obama administration threatened to block its weapons sales to Ankara unless Turkey became more conciliatory.[79] Somehow forgotten in all this soap-boxing was that the Gaza blockade was a violation of international law, the passengers on the Turkish-chartered vessel were unarmed, and at least one passenger, Turkish-American Furkan Dogan, died as a result of an Israeli bullet shot at point-black range at his face.[80] Perhaps if someone other than a Muslim had been killed, the international response would have been different.

Some European countries, too, have been cool to the changes in Turkey. On the face of it, Turkey is the perfect candidate for membership in the European Union. It has jumped through many of the requisite hoops, first applying to join the European Economic Community in 1959 and the European Union in 1987. It possesses the seventeenth top economy in the world and, according to Goldman Sachs, has a good shot at breaking into the top ten by 2050.[81] It occupies a vital crossroads between Europe, the Middle East, and Central Asia, bridging several civilizations even as it sits perched at the nexus of energy politics. If superpower status followed the rules of real estate—location, location, location—then Turkey would already be part of the EU. But Turkey is still waiting, and its prospects have only gotten dimmer in the last few years. Turkey is the only country in line for membership that has had two caveats attached to its application, that accession would be based on the EU's "absorptive capacity" and that Ankara might have to settle ultimately for something less than full membership.[82]

Opposition to Turkey's membership is heated. French and German leaders have spoken against accession, which mirrors the European public's point of view as well, for only 26 percent favors Turkish membership.[83] Though accession is not currently in the cards, the far right has united around a Europe-wide referendum to keep Turkey out of the European Union.[84] The general atmosphere of Islamophobia has poisoned Turkey's chances. Writes former European commissioner for external relations Chris Patten, "Conservative EU politicians admit privately that Turkey is more benefit than threat, but that to say so out loud would be political suicide."[85] Conservatives worry that, with membership, even more

Turks will find their way to western Europe, following the lead of other new EU citizens from east central Europe. "The Turks are conquering Germany in the same way the Kosovars conquered Kosovo: by using higher birthrates," argues Germany's Islamophobe du jour, Thilo Sarrazin, a member of Germany's Social Democratic Party.

The right wing has also raised the old specter of neo-Ottomanism, that Turkey is the advanced guard for radical Islam, sending immigrants to western Europe and eyeing its former territories in the Balkans. Bernard Lewis has even argued that Turkey's fundamentalism will strengthen to such an extent that, in a decade's time, it will resemble Iran, even as the Islamic Republic moves in the opposite direction.[86] For *New York Times* columnist Thomas Friedman, the process is already under way. He visited Istanbul in June 2010 to "find Turkey's Islamist government seemingly focused not on joining the European Union but the Arab League—no, scratch that, on joining the Hamas-Hezbollah-Iran resistance front against Israel."[87]

This is, however, a fundamental misunderstanding of the Justice and Development Party and its intentions. Radical Islam has about as much influence in modern-day Turkey as orthodox communism does in China. In both cases, what matters most is not ideology, but the political power of the ruling parties.[88] Economic growth, political stability, and soft-power diplomacy regularly trump ideological consistency. Turkey is becoming more nationalist and more assertive, but flexibility, not fundamentalism, has been the hallmark of its new foreign policy.[89] Turkey's turn toward the Middle East, Central Asia, and North Africa has followed the country's economic interests and has also in part been a reaction to the fading of the EU option. European assertions that Turks are not Europeans are having an obvious and possibly intended effect. Public support in Turkey for membership has declined from 70 percent in 2002 to below 48 percent today.[90]

In 1999, Bill Clinton suggested that if Ankara launched a reformist movement, the twenty-first century could be "Turkey's century."[91] Turkey has indeed heeded Clinton's advice. Now, Europe and the United States face a choice. If Washington works with Turkey as a partner, it has a far greater chance of resolving outstanding conflicts with Iran, inside Iraq, and between the Palestinians and Israelis, not to mention simmering disputes elsewhere in the Islamic world. If the European Union accepts Turkey as a member, its economic dynamism and new credibility in the Muslim world could help jolt Europe out of its current sclerosis. Spurned by one or both, Turkey's global influence will still grow, but Muslims the world over will interpret the rejection as just another example of Islamophobia.

The way Islamophobes consistently misrepresent the Justice and Development Party and Turkish society as becoming more extremist reveals their real anxieties. They're not worried here about al-Qaeda terrorism or even a Muslim Brotherhood style of politics. The Islamophobes of Europe are afraid of Turkey because it has successfully combined Islam with democracy and economic growth. As such, Turkey challenges all the stereotypes about Muslims and reveals the Islamophobic agenda for what it is: a new Crusade.

If Europe and the United States engage the new Turkey, they will discover a willing partner. More importantly, they will take the first step in ending Crusade 2.0.

Ending Crusade 2.0

Even in the middle of the Crusades, Muslims and Christians found ways of getting along. In the lands known as Outremer, where Christians established settlements in what is today the Middle East, the newcomers took on the habits of the locals. The Crusaders learned the languages of the area. They began to take baths—quite a novelty for the great European unwashed—and build according to the local traditions. They intermarried. "The native as well as the colonist has become polyglot and trust brings the most widely separated races together," wrote the historian Fulcher of Chartres around 1125. "The colonist has now become almost a native and the immigrant is one with the inhabitants."[1] In medieval al-Andalus, Jews and Christians lived in relative peace under Muslim rule, and a hybrid culture emerged that incubated Renaissance thinking and anticipated the Enlightenment. In the Ottoman Balkans too peasants appreciated the relative tolerance of the Ottomans: "Better the turban of the Turk than the tiara of the Pope," as they put it.[2]

To be sure, these were not idyllic times, simply periods

of comparative harmony in ages of war and intolerance. They suggest that conflicts between countries, religions, even civilizations are not inevitable. They remind us that the wars and intolerance of our present age can be overcome as well, just as the bloody wars between Persians and Arabs, between Protestants and Catholics, between Germans and French take place today almost exclusively in the pages of history books.

Promoting tolerance and understanding will not by itself prevent an even more violent upsurge of Islamophobia and a recrudescence of Crusade 2.0. Tolerance, after all, is often a rationale for the lack of engagement, for maintaining separate realms, for agreeing to disagree. Tolerance is: You have your Islamic tradition and we have our Judeo-Christian tradition and let's leave it at that. Tolerance is: Europe is uniquely Europe and Turkey is uniquely Turkey and never the twain shall meet in a common union. Tolerance is: We'll occupy your country and try not to disrupt your lives too much. Such tolerance is, of course, better than a ruthless crusade. But it is not true respect between equals.

Bridging the divide between Islam and the West—a divide patrolled by both the Taliban and Pamela Geller—will require bold engagement: "critique as well as dialogue, pressure as well as basic human respect, sticks such as sanctions as well as carrots such as better diplomatic and economic relations," as Juan Cole puts it.[3] Respect requires give and take, a willingness to change on both sides, and a capacity for self-criticism where appropriate. Even during the worst of the Crusades, Christians and Muslims in Outremer, al-Andalus, and the court of Frederick II found their way toward mutual respect.

Here are three concrete examples—cultural, political, and military—of putting such respect into practice today.

Going Back to Abraham

"Judeo-Christian" is a relatively recent construct. It emerged from the theological debates in Germany in the late-nineteenth century as a way of incorporating and belittling through hyphenation the Jewish contributions to Christian civilization.[4] Later, the term acquired its modern meaning of an equally shared tradition from Christian reformers hoping to counter the strain of anti-Jewish bigotry prevalent in the America of the 1920s. Prior to the twentieth century—and for much of that benighted era as well—Jews and Christians did not perceive such a shared tradition. "Jews regarded Christians as at best second-best and at worst as execrable idolaters, and Christians regarded Jews as at best worthy of conversion and at worst as deicides and antichrists," writes Jewish scholar Arthur Cohen.[5]

With this new "Judeo-Christian" construct, Jews were invited into the dominant culture much as Italians and Irish were ultimately redefined as white in postbellum America. Those who remained excluded from the club were the intended target of the gesture. From the 1970s on, U.S. conservatives and the Christian right increasingly embraced "Judeo-Christian" to emphasize their support of Israel against the Arabs. "'Why do they hate us so much?'"

General William Boykin asked the congregation in his famous 2003 sermon. "Ladies and gentlemen, the answer to that is because we're a Christian nation, because our foundation and our roots are Judeo-Christian. Did I say Judeo-Christian? Yes. Judeo-Christian. That means we've got a commitment to Israel."[6] (Similar language can be found in Europe where philosopher Jürgen Habermas has written of "apologists" for the national culture who "appeal to the 'Judeo-Christian tradition,' which distinguishes 'us' from the foreigners."[7])

But as historian Richard Bulliet points out, Islam and Christianity have at least as good a claim to hyphenated coexistence as Judaism and Christianity. The overlap of scriptures, the shared cultures in Outremer and al-Andalus, the similar struggles with modernity: these constitute an important history that can be drawn upon. Bulliet prefers to view Christianity and Islam as sometimes contentious siblings, as "two versions of the same socio-religious system."[8]

In 1076, some twenty years before the First Crusade, Pope Gregory VII sent a letter to the Muslim emir of Mauretania in which he wrote of the common Abrahamic traditions of the two religions.[9] Interfaith dialogue between the monotheisms often begins with an invocation of Abraham, a prophet in all three faiths and a prominent figure in the Qur'an. Of course, Gregory was also a key player in the transition from the peacemaking efforts of the tenth and eleventh centuries to the Christian militarism that produced the Crusades.[10] Still, holy war and holy peace were both options at the time, just as their secular versions are choices we face today.

The inclusion of Islam in the larger Abrahamic tradition is important for political reasons not just as a prerequisite for an interfaith dialogue (which ideally would go beyond these three monotheisms to include Buddhism, Hinduism, even secular humanism).[11] Too often, Boykin and the Christian right invoke the "Judeo-Christian" tradition to cast the current conflicts in the Middle East in apocalyptic language. Only when the monotheistic traditions sit down as cousins of equal stature, rather than Jews and Christians on one side against Muslims on the other, will the countries in the region achieve a just peace—and thereby remove one of the chief motivating factors for Crusade 2.0.

Ending Occupation

In one of his frequent over-the-top speculations, Islamophobe-in-chief Robert Spencer asks, "Will tourists in the year 2109 visit the Eiffel Minaret in Paris and the Westminster Mosque in London?"[12] It's a common refrain that goes back many centuries. The eighteenth-century historian Edward Gibbon, in a counterfactual aside, mused that if Charles Martel hadn't defeated the Saracens in the Battle of Tours, students at Oxford would be scrutinizing the Qur'an rather than the Bible.[13] The odd part of this anxiety over Muslim influence is that when both Spencer and Gibbon were penning their words, it was *their* countries that occupied Muslim lands not the other way around. In the

1770s, the British East India Company was consolidating its power in Bengal, which would become one of the great sources of plunder for the British Empire. In the twentieth century, meanwhile, the United States was occupying Afghanistan and Iraq.

Stalin, who knew a thing or two about atrocities, once said that the death of one man is a tragedy while the death of a million is a statistic. In the Islamophobia debates, the attack on a single Qur'an is a tragedy while the attack on millions of Muslims is a foreign policy. In our disgust over daily examples of Islam-bashing, we shouldn't lose sight of the larger context. As during the Crusades, the West has justified war and occupation by playing up the threat of Islam storming the battlements and profaning sacred sites. We have continued these wars and occupations even though they encourage the very reactions they are designed to suppress. "The terror from above will replenish the source of all terror from below: unhealed wounds," novelist Martin Amis observed in one of his less Islamophobic moments.[14] The humiliations caused by Crusade 1.0—the sacks of Jerusalem and Alexandria, the expropriation of resources during the colonial period, and the forced secularization by Westernizers like Ataturk—have buried deep into the cultures of the victims. The rise of Arab nationalism and political Islam, despite their mutual hostility, were both assertions of pride in the face of these historic impositions.

"They hate our freedoms—our freedom of religion, our freedom of speech, our freedom to vote and assemble and disagree with each other," George W. Bush said in his

September 20, 2001 address to Congress. No, they hate us—our governments—for *depriving* them of these freedoms by sending in troops, supporting authoritarian leaders, siding with Israel instead of even-handedly facilitating Middle East peace. As the Arab Spring has demonstrated, the public in the Muslim world embraces the rights to gather freely and speak freely. These events didn't happen *because* of U.S. policy but *despite* it. Washington favors stability above all, because the status quo is both predictable and favorable to the United States. This explains the double standard of supporting democracy in Iraq but not Saudi Arabia.

Realists worry that if the United States withdraws troops, the center will not hold and things will fall apart.[15] This has been the rationale for occupation put forward by every empire throughout history. The United States makes the same arguments for its huge Pacific military presence, its creation of the Africa Command, its policing of its "backyard" in Latin America and the Caribbean. Chaos is certainly one possible scenario following imperial withdrawal. Population transfer and communal violence, alas, was one part of India's immediate postcolonial history. But chaos did not ensue, for instance, when the Soviet Union withdrew from the Baltic states. An essential requirement of democracy, the promotion of which has been the official rationale for U.S. nation-building exercises, is the end of occupation.

The same holds true for the major U.S. ally in the Middle East, Israel, in its relationship with Palestinians.

Israeli settlement policies—its ongoing annexation of Palestinian land and military occupation of Palestinian towns and cities—have been one of the core obstacles to Middle East peace and to the development of a fair and just democracy in Israel. The establishment of a viable Palestinian state that coexists peacefully with Israel is a prerequisite for ending Crusade 2.0, for the Israeli-Palestinian divide is one of the great unresolved issues of the Cold War. The United States cannot by itself push the restart button on its relationship with the Muslim world. Israel too must be part of this reengagement process. There can be no peace through occupation.

Peter Beinart, the *jihad* liberal who channeled the spirit of Truman in supporting the Iraq War, eventually came to regret that decision. After throwing his lot in with the Bush team, Beinart discovered that Arthur Schlesinger, Francis Fukuyama, and even Jeanne Kirkpatrick all had doubts about U.S. occupation strategy. Second thoughts ensued. To attempt to sustain the unipolar moment through aggressive unilateralism, he concludes in his book-length apologia *The Icarus Syndrome*, is the essence of hubris: "A wise foreign policy starts with the recognition that since America's power is limited, we must limit our enemies."[16] Our occupation policies are woefully expensive—$3 trillion for the war in Iraq alone, a $1.2 trillion annual national security budget that supports the infrastructure of occupation, about $3 billion in annual military assistance to Israel that helps that country maintain its aggressive settlement policies—and particularly so at a time of economic crisis.[17] As importantly, these policies sustain the very enemies they are supposed to eliminate. Ending this addiction to occupation is an essential military transformation needed to end Crusade 2.0.

Embracing Turkey

Over the summer of 2010, British prime minister David Cameron wanted to be very clear. Israel's attack on the Turkish flotilla the previous May was "unacceptable." And his European colleagues who opposed Turkish membership in the EU were simply wrong, just as wrong as French president Charles de Gaulle had been to oppose British membership in the 1960s. "We know what it is like to be shut out of the club," Cameron said.[18]

What Cameron didn't say was that the club was in trouble. Greece and Ireland were in an economic tailspin. Spain too had seen its booming economy come to a crashing halt. And the rest of Europe feared that it would be dragged down into the morass by its single currency, like an entire group of attached mountaineers pulled from the cliff face by the fall of a couple climbers.[19] In December 2010, the foreign ministers of Britain, Finland, Sweden, and Italy issued their version of a "dear colleague" letter urging EU membership for Turkey. They sounded a note of quiet desperation, however. "New members can help Europe return to economic dynamism and take on its proper weight in world affairs," they wrote.[20]

Because of French and German opposition and the mythmaking of Islamophobes, Turkey remains in the European halfway house. Despite what Thomas Friedman and others have predicted, the ruling party has not taken a major detour. Rather, the Justice and Development Party has expanded on the political and economic changes initiated by Prime Minister Turgut Ozal in the 1980s. French and German leaders might be cool to Turkish accession to the EU, but the Justice and Development Party continues to push through its reform agenda with one eye on Europe. A referendum that passed by a large margin in September 2010 gave the civilian government more power to shoulder the military out of politics and implement policies to strengthen gender equality, expand collective bargaining rights, and effect other changes necessary to smooth the way for EU membership.[21]

Turkey still has a considerable way to go, and there have been setbacks, particularly regarding minority rights for Kurds and others. But as the accession negotiations with Romania and Bulgaria demonstrated, the carrot of EU membership can accelerate liberal reforms like nothing else. But the carrot has to be real and not simply a mirage.

Taking Turkey seriously is part of taking multiculturalism seriously. European countries have been slow to acknowledge that they are no longer unitary cultures. The backlash against immigrants, and Muslims in particular, has been intense. But no one promised that diversity would be achieved by holding hands in a circle and singing reassuring jingles. In the past, European countries achieved a measure of homogeneity through war, genocide, and the forced homogenization of the army, the school, and the church. Those options are fortunately no longer available, however much the extreme right hungers for the "good old days."

In an Europe of declining birth rates and stagnating economies, multiculturalism is an indispensable asset, whether it involves embracing the dynamism of immigrants or the dynamism of Turkey. This vision does not imply a future of assimilation, in which immigrants and Turkey give up their identities, become Christians, and dissolve into some bland EuroWorld. The countries of Europe have fought to retain their national cultures within the EU; the Catalans and Welsh and Bretons have worked hard to preserve their own cultures within those nation-states. In the same way, immigrants and Turkey bring something to the European table that makes it a more interesting and lively and prosperous space.

As the first German president to address the Turkish parliament, Christian Wulff got it exactly right in his 2010 speech: because of immigrants, Germany was "more diverse, open and connected to the world."[22] Europe can reap the same benefits by bringing Turkey into the EU.

Whither Crusade 2.0?

Several prominent Americans took strong stances against Islamophobia in 2010. New York Mayor Michael Bloomberg took a potentially career-killing position in favor of Park51. *Newsweek* international editor Fareed Zakaria returned his award from the Anti-Defamation League because of its opposition to the cultural center.[23]

But one of the strongest denunciations in the United States came from an unlikely source: TV anchor Katie Couric. "The bigotry expressed against Muslims in this country has been one of the most disturbing stories to surface this year," she said in her 2010 round-up. Her recommendation for addressing the problem was rather subversive: a Muslim version of *The Cosby Show*. That show, she explained, "did so much to change attitudes about African-Americans in this country, and I think sometimes people are afraid of what they don't understand."[24]

It was certainly an interesting proposal. Given the TV industry's constant search for new niche markets and the relative wealth of the Muslim community in the United States, a Muslim *Cosby Show* is no doubt already in the planning stages.

But *The Cosby Show*, which premiered in 1984 and ran until 1992, was not the starting point of the campaign to roll back racism in the United States. It was made possible only by the efforts of many preceding movements stretching back to the abolitionists, the Harlem Renaissance, the campaigns against Jim Crow, and ultimately the civil rights movement of the 1960s. These social movements challenged the institutional discrimination against African Americans. They broke down the barriers that kept African Americans on the fringes of radio, film, and TV. They changed structures, and American attitudes gradually changed to keep up.

Americans certainly could use more information about Islam. But more information alone, in our world of information overload, is not going to eliminate Islamophobia. As the original Crusaders streamed back from the Muslim world, they brought with them much more information about Islam.[25] But more information didn't prompt the Europeans to rethink their holy war. That's because Europeans continued to view Islam through a distorted lens and act accordingly. Those distortions—that Muslims are inherently violent, duplicitous, and imperialistic—continue today. A TV show about "good Muslims" won't necessarily change viewers' attitudes about "bad Muslims," and it will simply reinforce the notion that the West determines who is and is not the right kind of Muslim.

After all, it's not really about Muslims. It's about us, the West, the non-Muslim West. We have yet to come to terms with the Crusades that still reside so deeply within our own hearts, with the Cold War categories that still shape our thinking, and with our desire to intervene and control events in the Muslim world. We have to listen to Islam—not just the religion but the resistance as well.[26] The motivation behind political Islam is justice. Islamists decry the corruption, lawlessness, and economic inequalities that they see in their own societies. They have also protested against Western policies—promoted by governments or international institutions—that have perpetuated these injustices.

We must distinguish between this resistance and the acts of al-Qaeda and its ilk. By addressing the underlying injustices, we can isolate and eventually close down al-Qaeda. By ending the wars of occupation, by reaching out to Turkey, by expanding our notions of an exclusive Judeo-Christian culture, we can change the structures that perpetuate injustice. As a result, Islamophobia—and anti-Western animus—will both disappear. Like an army that has run out of provisions and lost its way, Crusade 2.0 will grind to a halt, the last of its kind.

Timeline

1804- September, U.S. Commodore Edward Preble uses suicide bomb tactic

1830- Influx of Catholic immigrants into the America sparks the rise of a Protestant nativist movement

1922- French Orientalist Etienne Dinet coins the term "Islamophobia"

1924- Ataturk formally ends Islamic caliphate

1928- Hassan al-Banna founds Muslim Brotherhood

1941- Japanese Americans forced into internment camps in the wake of Pearl Harbor

1946- Winston Churchill's "Iron Curtain" speech; Cold War begins

1948- Israel founded

1951- CIA creates Crusade for Freedom

1952- Turkey inducted into NATO

1954- Bernard Lewis essay "Communism and Islam"

1957- al-Fatah founded by Palestinian nationalists

1960- OPEC founded

1964- Sayyid Qutb completes *Milestones*

1973- Yom Kippur War

1979- Soviet invasion of Afghanistan

1979- Overthrow of the shah in Iran

1982–1985- Hezbollah founded in Lebanon

1983- Beirut bombing

1985- Alex Odeh assassinated

1987- Hamas founded

1988- al-Qaeda founded in Afghanistan

1988- Salman Rushdie publishes *The Satanic Verses*, a novel that satirizes aspects of Islam

1989- First semi-free elections in Jordan, fall of the Berlin Wall, Tiananmen Square

1990- Iraq invades Kuwait

1990- The term "Islamo-facism" coined by Malise Ruthven

1991- January, Gulf War 1

1991- December, fall of the USSR

1991- December, Algerian civil war breaks out

1992- Hezbollah for the first time fields political candidates for political office

1993- Summer, Samuel Huntington publishes "Clash of Civilizations" article

1993- February, World Trade Center bombed

1993- October, Battle of Mogadishu

1994- Hebron Massacre by Baruch Goldstein

1995- August, NATO bombing of Bosnia and Herzegovina

1997- February, "soft coup" in Turkey ousts Islamist prime minister

1998- August, embassy bombings in Kenya and Tanzania

1999- March, NATO bombing of Yugoslavia

2000- October, USS *Cole* attacked

2000- March, Pope John Paul II apologizes for the Crusades

2001- October, U.S. commences military operations in Afghanistan

2001- September, 9/11

2001- September, Bush utilizes the word "Crusade" in a speech regarding the new war on terror

2001- September, in front of a mosque, Bush condemns attacks on American Muslims.

2001- October, USA PATRIOT Act passed

2002- David Project founded by Aubrey Chernick

2002- February, Bush again uses the word "Crusade" in a speech to U.S. troops in Alaska

2003- February, worldwide demonstrations against the impending invasion of Iraq

2003- March, U.S. invasion of Iraq

2003- June, Officers' Christian Fellowship sermon "warriors of God's Kingdom"

2003- September 23, launch of JihadWatch blog

2004- November, murder of Dutch filmmaker Theo van Gogh by a Dutch-Moroccan Muslim

2005- September, Danish newspaper *Jyllands-Posten* publishes unflattering cartoons about Islam

2005- October, George W. Bush introduces term "Islamofacism" in speech

2006- January, Hamas wins Gaza election

2006- September, Pope Benedict XVI speech at University of Regensburg

2006- December, U.S.-backed Ethiopian invasion of Somalia

2008- November, Obama elected 44th president of the U.S.

2009- Rise of the Tea Party movement in America

2009- June, Obama's Cairo speech

2009- November, Fort Hood shootings

2009- November, Switzerland bans construction of minarets, Muslim prayer towers

2010- May, Time Square bomb scare

2010- May, Gaza flotilla incident

2010- June-August, protests over construction of Park51

2010- July, Dove World Qur'an burning controversy begins

2010- August, release of Thilo Sarrazin's book *Germany Does Away with Itself*

2010- August, Tennessee proposes construction of mosque

2010- August, Bloomberg, Olbermann, Colbert, Stewart all condemn anti-Muslim hysteria

2010- November, Public Research Institute report shows 45% of Americans see Islam as at odds with American values

2010- November, Oklahoma "Save Our State" amendment banning shariah passed

2010- December, commencement of the Arab Spring

2011- January, Jared Loughner kills five people and almost assassinates Congressman Gabrielle Giffords

2011- March, congressional hearings on Muslim radicalization

2011- March, Herman Cain says Muslims would not be allowed in his cabinet

2011- April, French burqa ban goes into affect

2011- April, Obama releases birth certificate

2011- May, Osama bin Laden killed

2011- June, CAIR report "Same Hate, New Target"

2011- July, Norway shootings

2011- August, CAP report "Fear, Inc." published

2011- September, Park51 opens

Notes

Introduction

1. According to the Pew Global Attitudes Project, only 23 percent of Americans held unfavorable views toward Muslims in 2008, compared to 31 percent in 2004. Pew Global Attitudes Project, "Unfavorable Views of Both Jews and Muslims Increase in Europe," Pew Research Center, September 17, 2008, http://pewresearch.org/pubs/955/ unfavorable-views-of-both-jews-and-muslims-increase-in-europe.

2. "Same Hate, Different Target" *Council on American Islamic Relations* (Washington, DC, December 2009–January 2010), 22.

3. Ibid. 53–54.

4. Tim O'Leary, "Temecula Mosque Proposal Targeted in Pending Protest," *Valley News*, July 23, 2010, http://www.myvalleynews.com/ story/49601/.

5. Stephanie Rice, "'Anti-Islamic' Bus Ads Appear in Major Cities," *Christian Science Monitor*, July 28, 2010, http://www.csmonitor.com/USA/ Society/2010/0728/Anti-Islamic-bus-ads-appear-in-major-cities.

6. *Sharia* is actually divine law, in contrast to *fiqh*, which is more literally Islamic law. John Esposito and Dalia Mogahed compare *sharia* to a compass and *fiqh* to a map. "This map must conform to the compass, but it reflects different times, places and geography. The compass is fixed; the map is subject to change." John Esposito and Dalia Mogahed, *Who Speaks for Islam?* (New York: Gallup Press, 2007), 53.

7. "Limbaugh Calls Islamic Center a 'Victory Monument at Ground Zero,'" *Media Matters*, August 17, 2010, http://mediamatters.org/ mmtv/201008170036.

8. "Right-wing Media Blast President Obama's Support for Freedom of Religion," *Media Matters*, August 14, 2010.

9. Only 30 percent of Americans viewed Islam positively that summer, a rather significant drop from 2005 when an already low 41 percent of Americans had a favorable opinion of the religion. Pew Forum on Religion and Public Life, "Public Remains Conflicted Over Islam," Pew Research Center, August 24, 2010, http://pewresearch.org/pubs/1706/ poll-americans-views-of-muslims-object-to-new-york-islamic-center-islam-violence. Polling from the *Washington Post*/ABC supports these numbers as well. According to a September 2010 report, "49 percent of all Americans say they have generally unfavorable opinions of Islam, compared with 37 percent who say they have favorable ones. That's the most negative split on the question in *Post*-ABC polls dating to

October 2001." Jon Cohen and Kyle Dropp, "Most Americans Object to Planned Islamic Center Near Ground Zero, Poll Finds," *Washington Post*, September 9, 2010, http://www.washingtonpost.com/wp-dyn/content/article/2010/09/08/AR2010090806231.html.

10. Bobby Ghosh, "Mosque Controversy: Does America Have a Muslim Problem?" *Time*, August 19, 2010. http://www.time.com/time/magazine/article/0,9171,2011936,00.html; Bobby Ghosh, "Is America Islamophobic," *Time*, August 30, 2010, http://www.time.com/time/covers/0,16641,20100830,00.html.

11 . Kevin Sieff, "Florida Pastor Terry Jones's Koran Burning Has Far-Reaching Effect," *Washington Post*, April 2, 2011, http://www.washingtonpost.com/local/education/florida-pastor-terry-joness-koran-burning-has-far-reaching-effect/2011/04/02/AFpiFoQC_story.html.

12. Wajahat Ali, Eli Clifton, Matthew Duss, Lee Fang, Scott Keyes, and Faiz Shakir, *Fear, Inc.* (Washington, DC: Center for American Progress, August 26, 2011).

13. Alex Altman, "TIME Poll: Majority Oppose Mosque, Many Distrust Muslims," *Time*, August 19, 2010, http://www.time.com/time/nation/article/0,8599,2011799,00.html#ixzz1ACL7hA6g.

14. There are 1.57 billion Muslims in the world, according to a 2009 Pew Forum report. See Richard Alan Greene, "Nearly 1 in 4 people Worldwide is Muslim, Report Says," CNN, October 7, 2009, http://articles.cnn.com/2009-10-07/world/muslim.world.population_1_god-but-god-middle-east-distant?_s=PM:WORLD.

15. Alexander Cockburn, "The Tenth Crusade," *CounterPunch*, September 7, 2002, http://www.counterpunch.org/cockburn0907.html. There is some controversy over the number of crusades, with Frederick II and Louis IX either launching two crusades apiece or a single, multistage crusade each. This puts the number of crusades at either seven or nine. Some scholars, like Christopher Tyerman, even consider the seventeenth-century war of the Holy League against the Ottoman Empire to be a crusade. Christopher Tyerman, *God's War* (Cambridge, MA: Harvard University Press, 2006), 914.

16. Figures as of October 2, 2011. See "The Year of the Drone," *New America Foundation* http://counterterrorism.newamerica.net/drones.

17. Pew Global Attitudes Project, "Obama More Popular Abroad Than At Home, Global Image of U.S. Continues to Benefit," Pew Research Center, June 17, 2010, http://pewglobal.org/2010/06/17/obama-more-popular-abroad-than-at-home/.

18. "Obama/Muslims," *Newsweek* poll, August 27. 2010, http://nw-assets.s3.amazonaws.com/pdf/1004-ftop.pdf.

19. Juan Cole, *Engaging the Muslim World* (New York: Palgrave/MacMillan, 2009), 1.

20. Frank Rich, "How Fox Betrayed Petraeus," *New York Times*, August 21, 2010. http://www.nytimes.com/2010/08/22/opinion/22rich. html?_r=1.

21. Frank Lambert, *The Barbary Wars* (New York: Hill and Wang, 2005), 8. Interview with Raed Jarrar on November 5, 2010 (Washington, DC), http://www.fpif.org/articles/ interview_with_raed_jarrar_and_niki_akhavan.

22. Frank Lambert, *The Barbary Wars*. The full quote is: "Jihad and the rifle alone: no negotiations, no conferences and no dialogues." Quoted in John Esposito, *The Future of Islam* (New York: Oxford University Press, 2010), 68.

23. Jocelyn Cesari, "Islamophobia in the West" in John Esposito and Ibrahim Kalin, eds. *Islamophobia* (New York: Oxford University Press, 2011), 21. *Islamophobia: A Challenge for Us All* (London: Runnymede Trust, 1997).

24. Martin Amis, *The Second Plane* (New York: Knopf, 2008), x.

25. Laura Clark and Tahira Yaqoob, "Martin Amis Launches Fresh Attack on Muslim Faith Saying Islamic States Are 'Less Evolved,'" *Daily Mail*, October 18, 2006, http://www.dailymail.co.uk/news/article-488239/ Martin-Amis-launches-fresh-attack-Muslim-faith-saying-Islamic-states- evolved.html.

26. Wafa Sultan, *A God Who Hates* (New York: St. Martin's, 2009), 240.

27. Irshad Manji, *The Trouble with Islam* (New York: St. Martin's, 2003).

28. Nonie Darwish, *Now They Call Me Infidel* (New York: Penguin, 2006), 197.

29. Mahmood Mamdani, *Good Muslim, Bad Muslim* (New York: Pantheon, 2004), 18.

30. Paul Berman, for instance, devotes much of his book *The Flight of the Intellectuals* to an attack against Ian Buruma and Timothy Garten-Ash, liberals both, who have taken more nuanced approaches to the issue of political Islam. Paul Berman, *The Flight of the Intellectuals* (Brooklyn: Melville House, 2010).

31. For excellent introductions to Islam, I recommend John Esposito's *The Future of Islam* (New York: Oxford University Press, 2010) and Reza Aslan's *No God but God* (New York: Random House, 2005).

32. For the story of Abdul Ghaffar Khan, see Amitabh Pal, *"Islam" Means Peace* (New York: Praeger, 2011).

33. Edward Said, *Covering Islam* (New York: Vintage, 1997), xvi.

34. A short list of Muslim statements against terrorism can be found here: http://www.unc.edu/~kurzman/terror.htm.

35. Nicholas Kristof deserves mention in this regard for his op-ed "Message to Muslims: I'm Sorry," *New York Times*, September 18, 2010.

Chapter One

1. *The Song of Roland* (New York: Penguin, 1983), 8.

2. Three hundred years later, the politics of Iberia remained extraordinarily complex. Another representative figure in this regard is El Cid, an eleventh-century Spanish nobleman and the hero of a twelfth-century epic poem. El Cid commanded both Muslim and Christian armies and, under Alfonso VI, a combined force that he used to create his own principality within the Moorish realm of Valencia.

3. "Historians have even speculated that had the Carolingian empire existed longer, the Christian and the Islamic cultures might have been on better terms." Tomaz Mastnak, *Crusading Peace* (Berkeley, CA: University of California Press, 2002), 67–68.

4. For an in-depth exploration of the Battle of Roncevaux, see David Levering Lewis, *God's Crucible* (New York: Norton, 2008), 245ff.

5. Marco Polo, Peter Harris, Colin Thubron, William Marsden, and Thomas Wright. *The Travels of Marco Polo, the Venetian* (New York: Alfred A. Knopf, 2008), 130.

6. Max Weber, *Economy and Society: An Outline of Interpretive Sociology, Volume 2* (Berkeley, University of California Press, 1978), 574.

7. And earlier: The ninth century Christian chronicler Eulogius depicted Mohammed as the Antichrist and his followers as inherently violent. John Tolan, *Saracens* (New York: Columbia University Press, 2002), 94.

8. Robert the Monk in Dana C. Munro, "Urban and the Crusaders," *Translations and Reprints from the Original Sources of European History*, Vol. 1:2 (Philadelphia: University of Pennsylvania, 1895), 5–8. http://www.fordham.edu/halsall/source/urban2-5vers.html. No original versions of Pope Urban II's famous speech exist, so we must rely on a number of versions compiled by contemporary eyewitnesses.

9. Quoted in Karen Armstrong, "We Cannot Afford to Maintain These Ancient Prejudices against Islam," *Guardian*, September 18, 2006, http://www.guardian.co.uk/commentisfree/2006/sep/18/religion.catholicism.

10. *The Qur'an* (New York: Penguin, 1981), 321 (Repentance 9:5).

11. In practice, Islam would eventually accommodate quite well with polytheists, as the Mughal Empire demonstrated in India when Muslim-Hindu relations prospered under the rule of Akbar.

12. *The Qur'an*, 361 (The Cow 2:256)

13. "Muslim law eventually expanded on these prohibitions [of killing women, children, monks, rabbis, the elderly and other noncombatants] to outlaw the torture of prisoners of war; the mutilation of the dead; rape, molestation, or any kind of sexual violence during combat; the killing of diplomats, the wanton destruction of property, and the demolition of religious or medical institutions—regulations that, as Hilmi Zawati has observed, were all eventually incorporated into the modern international laws of war." Reza Aslan, *No God but God*, 84.

14. Ayesha Jalal, *Partisans of Allah* (Cambridge, MA: Harvard University Press, 2008), 7; Khaled Abou El Fadl et al., *The Place of Tolerance in Islam* (Boston: Beacon, 2002), 102.

15. See discussion in Malise Ruthven, "The Birth of Islam: A Different View," *New York Review of Books*, April 7, 2011, 82.

16. *The Jerusalem Bible* (New York: Doubleday, 1968), 310–11 (1 Samuel 15).

17. *The Jerusalem Bible*, 336 (Revelations 19:11).

18. Steven Runciman, *The First Crusade* (New York: Cambridge University Press, 2005), 48–49.

19. Karen Armstrong, *Holy War* (New York: Doubleday, 1992), 179. Later scholarship has challenged these numbers as too high, but contemporary chroniclers described an atrocity that had considerable impact on both sides.

20. Christopher Tyerman, *God's War* (Cambridge, MA: Harvard University Press, 2006), 158.

21. Amin Maalouf, *The Crusades through Arab Eyes* (New York: Schocken Books, 1985), xiv.

22. Karen Armstrong, *Holy War*, 65.

23. According to Fulcher of Chartres, Pope Urban II alluded to the spotty records of many of the Crusaders when he proclaimed at the Council of Clermont: "Let those who for a long time have been robbers, now become knights. Let those who have been fighting against their brothers and relatives now fight in a proper way against the barbarians." Quoted in Graham Fuller, *A World without Islam* (New York: Little, Brown, 2010), 98.

24. Ibid., 72–73.

25. Colin Wells, *Sailing to Byzantium* (New York: Random House, 2006), 33.

26. Daniel Baraz, *Medieval Cruelty* (Ithaca, NY: Cornell University Press, 2003), 87–88.

27. Amin Maalouf, *The Crusades through Arab Eyes*, 199.

28. Karen Armstrong, *Holy War*, 260.

29. Ibid., 453.

30. It also recalled what happened in the seventh century when the Persians seized Antioch and Damascus and Jews slaughtered thousands of Christians throughout Mesopotamia to exact revenge for 300 years of persecution. David Levering Lewis, *God's Crucible*, 60.

31. *The Qur'an*, 157 (Counsel 42:40).

32. Few in the West complained later when, at the Battle of Ain Jalut, the Mameluke general Baibars defeated the marauding Mongols, saving not only Islam but Christian Europe as well. Karen Armstrong, *Holy War*, 447.

33. Jack Goody, *Islam in Europe* (London: Polity, 2004), 63.

34. Amin Malouf, *The Crusades through Arab Eyes*, 54.

35. Goody, *Islam in Europe*, 29.

36. The Muslim world was at least four centuries more advanced than the Europeans in the eighth century, argues historian David Levering Lewis, *God's Crucible*, 286. He writes, further, that "the victory of Charles the Hammer must be seen as greatly contributing to the creation of an economically retarded, balkanized, fratricidal Europe that, in defining itself in opposition to Islam made virtues out of religious persecution, cultural particularism, and hereditary aristocracy." David Levering Lewis, *God's Crucible*, 174.

37. Amin Maalouf, *The Crusades through Arab Eyes*, 39

38. The great historian of the Byzantine era Stephen Runciman writes that the destruction of Alexandria was rivaled only by the atrocities committed against Jerusalem in 1099 and Constantinople in 1204. "Alexandria's wealth had been phenomenal," he writes, "and the victors were maddened at the sight of so much booty. They spared no one. The native Christians and the Jews suffered as much as the Muslims; and even the European merchants settled in the city saw their factories and storehouses ruthlessly looted." Stephen Runciman, *A History of the Crusades, Volume 3* (Cambridge: Cambridge University Press, 1951),446.

39. Quoted in Christopher Tyerman, *God's War*, xiv.

40. Quoted in Karen Armstrong, *Holy War*, 207.

41. Tariq Ali, *The Clash of Fundamentalisms* (New York: Verso, 2002), 39–40.

42. Bernard Lewis, *Faith and Power* (New York: Oxford University Press, 2010), 15.

43. Christopher Tyerman, *God's War*, 638.

44. John Tolan, *Saracens*, 211.

45. Christopher Tyerman, *God's War*, 102.

46. Karen Armstrong, *Holy War*, 178.

47. Such positive assessments are rare today. When Bill Maher cited the courage of the 9/11 attackers on *Politically Incorrect*, ABC cancelled his

show for being politically incorrect in all the wrong ways. Maher said: "We have been the cowards. Lobbing cruise missiles from two thousand miles away. That's cowardly. Staying in the airplane when it hits the building. Say what you want about it. Not cowardly." Though, as Susan Faludi points out, the vehemence of the denunciations of Maher did not compare to what pundits said about Susan Sontag, who published less provocative remarks in a *New Yorker* article. See Susan Faludi, *The Terror Dream* (New York: MacMillan, 2007), 28.

48. Luther was actually of two minds, declaring Turks and Catholics to be the Antichrist at one point and then, at another, arguing that the Turk "is far too gross, his devilish ways far too obvious" to qualify as the true Antichrist. See Paul Levin, *Turkey and the European Union* (New York: Palgrave MacMillan, 2011), 107.

49. Tomaz Mastnak, "Europe and the Muslims: The Permanent Crusade?" in Emran Qureshi and Michael Sells, *The New Crusades* (New York: Columbia University Press, 2003), 225. Of course, if Turkey renounced Islam and adopted Christianity, Penn's Europe would welcome the country into its association. See Bernard Lewis, *Faith and Power*, 37.

50. Quoted in John Esposito, *The Islamic Threat* (NY: Oxford University Press, 1999), 44. For other Orientalist stereotypes, see Edward Said, *Orientalism* (New York: Vintage, 1979).

51. For instance, in *The Song of Roland*, the Saracens appear as polytheists, praying to Apollo and the pagan goddess Termagant. In fact, the army of the caliph contained many different peoples, including Slavs and black Africans, who indeed worshipped a variety of gods. At the time, moreover, Christian Europe faced many pagan enemies on its frontiers, so polytheism was as great if not greater a threat than Islam. Jo Ann Hoeppner Moran Cruz, "Popular Attitudes towards Islam in Medieval Europe," in David Blanks and Michael Frassetto, eds. *Western Views of Islam in Medieval and Early Modern Europe* (New York: St. Martin's Press, 1999), 57–59.

52. Ibid., 68.

53. "Pat Robertson Claimed That Islam 'at Its Core, Teaches Violence,'" *Media Matters*, July 18, 2005, http://mediamatters.org/mmtv/200507180003.

54. Jerry Curry, "Islam is a Violent Religion," *WebToday*, September 11, 2010, http://www.audacityofhypocrisy.com/2010/09/11/islam-is-a-violent-religion-by-maj-general-jerry-curry-us-army-ret/.

55. After the comments generated intense reactions—and riots—around the world, Falwell apologized for his comments. Mary Jayne McKay, "Falwell Sorry for Bashing Muhammed," *CBS News*, October 14, 2002,

http://www.cbsnews.com/stories/2002/10/11/60minutes/main525316.
shtml.

56. "Pope 'Sorry' for Offense to Islam," *BBC News*, September 16, 2006,
http://news.bbc.co.uk/2/hi/5351988.stm.

57. Akbar S. Ahmed, "Bridgebuilder to the Muslim World," *beliefnet*, April
2005, http://www.beliefnet.com/Faiths/Islam/2005/04/Bridge-Builder-
To-The-Muslim-World.aspx.

58. Christopher Caldwell, *Reflections on the Revolution in Europe* (New York:
Doubleday, 2009), 187.

59. Bernard Lewis, "The Roots of Muslim Rage," *Atlantic*, September
1990, http://www.theatlantic.com/magazine/archive/1990/09/
the-roots-of-muslim-rage/4643/.

60. Samuel Huntington, *The Clash of Civilizations and the Remaking of the
World Order* (New York: Simon and Schuster, 1996), 258.

61. And other crimes followed: the 10/12 attacks in Bali in 2002, the 5/16
suicide bombings in Casablanca in 2003, the 3/11 train bombing in
Madrid in 2004, and the 7/7 bombings in London in 2005.

62. "A Dossier of Civilian Casualties in Iraq 2003–2005," *Iraq Body Count*,
July 19, 2005, http://www.iraqbodycount.org/analysis/reference/
press-releases/12/.

63. David Brown, "Study Claims Iraq's 'Excess' Death Toll Has
Reached 655,000," *Washington Post*, October 11, 2006, http://
www.washingtonpost.com/wp-dyn/content/article/2006/10/10/
AR2006101001442.html.

64. Carl Conetta, *Strange Victory* (Boston: Project on Defense Alternatives,
2002), http://www.comw.org/pda/0201strangevic.html.

65. Stephen Walt, "Why They Hate Us II," *Foreign Policy*, November 30,
2009, http://walt.foreignpolicy.com/posts/2009/11/30/why_they_hate_
us_ii_how_many_muslims_has_the_us_killed_in_the_past_30_years.

66. Ali Sina, "Is Political Islam Fascist?" in *Beyond Jihad*, Kim Ezra
Shienbaum and Jamal Hasan, eds. (Bethesda, MD: Academica Press,
2006), 113.

67. Justin Elliott, "How the 'Ground Zero Mosque' Fear Mongering
Began," *Salon*, August 16, 2010, http://www.salon.com/news/politics/
war_room/2010/08/16/ground_zero_mosque_origins.

68. Reza Aslan, *No God but God*, 248; Daniel Pipes, *Militant Islam Reaches
America* (New York: Norton, 2002), xiv; Vali Nasr, *The Shia Revival* (New
York: Norton, 2006).

69. William Pfaff, "Manufacturing Insecurity," *Foreign Affairs*, November/
December 2010, 136.

70. See Eliza Griswold, *The Tenth Parallel* (New York: Farrar, Straus, Giroux, 2010), 90–91.

71. David Belden, "Backward Christian Soldiers," *Humanist*, January/February 2008, http://newhumanist.org.uk/1681/backward-christian-soldiers; Boykin quote from Peter Gottschalk and Gabriel Greenberg, *Islamophobia* (Lanham: Rowman and Littlefield, 2008), 13.

72. Quoted in John Esposito, *The Future of Islam* (Oxford, 2010), 20. Or, as Ann Coulter put, "We should invade their countries, kill their leaders and convert them to Christianity." Ann Coulter, "This Is War," *National Review*, September 13, 2001, http://old.nationalreview.com/coulter/coulter.shtml.

73. Consider also the concept of *taqiyya*. "The term *Taqiyya*, caution, precaution, denotes an Islamic concept of dispensation—the idea that under compulsion or menace, a believer may be dispensed from fulfilling certain conditions of religion," writes Bernard Lewis. Bernard Lewis, *The Assassins* (New York: Basic, 2002), 25. Islamophobes have taken the concept and run with it. As Wafa Sultan asserts, a Muslim conceals "his true feelings and cherished beliefs when he feels that non-Muslims around him have the upper hand, while at the same time working secretly to achieve his great objective, so that he can attack them when the time is ripe." Wafa Sultan, *A God Who Hates*, 242. But the concept of *taqiyya* means something quite different in the Islamic tradition: the Qur'an says that believers, if they or their loved ones are in extreme danger, can conceal their faith. In sixteenth-century Spain, *taqiyya* was the only way to survive when the crown offered the choice of conversion, expulsion, or death.

74. Quoted in Daniel Varisco, "Inventing Islamism," in Richard Martin and Abbas Barzegar, *Islamism* (Stanford: Stanford University Press, 2010), 37.

75. Quoted in Daniel Pipes, *Militant Islam Reaches America*, 46.

76. Edward Cline, "The Fascists in Our Midst," Center for the Advancement of Capitalism, August 15, 2006, http://www.capitalismcenter.org/Philosophy/Commentary/06/08-15-06.htm.

77. "What Should be Done with Iran?; First Muslim Congressman Speaks Out," CNN, November 14, 2006. http://transcripts.cnn.com/TRANSCRIPTS/0611/14/gb.01.html.

78. Frank Newport, "Republicans and Democrats Disagree on Muslim Hearings," Gallup, March 9, 2011, http://www.gallup.com/poll/146540/Republicans-Democrats-Disagree-Muslim-Hearings.aspx.

79. See, for example, Norman Daniel, *Islam and the West* (Oxford: OneWorld Publications, 1993), 100ff.

80. Robert Spencer, *The Truth about Muhammad* (Washington, DC: Regnery, 2006).

81. Daniel, *Islam and the West*,16.

Chapter Two

1. Blanche Wiesen Cook, *The Declassified Eisenhower* (New York: Doubleday, 1981), 131–32.

2. Christopher Caldwell, *Reflections on the Revolution in Europe*, 281.

3. Bernard Lewis, "Communism and Islam," in Walter Laqueur, *The Middle East in Transition* (Freeport, NY: Books for Libraries Press, 1971), 320.

4. Richard Bulliet, *The Case for Islamo-Christian Civilization* (New York: Columbia University Press, 2004), 100.

5. Stephen Kinzer, *Reset* (New York: Times Books, 2010),145–150. Here, the United States was merely following the footsteps of the British, who supported the Saudis in their struggle against the Ottoman Empire.

6. Robert Dreyfuss, *Devil's Game* (New York: Metropolitan, 2005).

7. Graham Fuller, *A World without Islam*, 263.

8. Dreyfuss, *Devil's Game*, 125.

9. Ibid. 277.

10. Paul Kennedy, *The Rise and Fall of Great Powers* (New York: Random House, 1987); Francis Fukuyama, *The End of History and the Last Man* (New York: Avon, 1992); Charles Krauthammer, "The Unipolar Moment," *Foreign Affairs*, 70, no. 1 (1990–91).

11. Samuel Huntington, *Who Are We?* (New York: Simon & Schuster, 2004), 262.

12. Interview with Phyllis Bennis, February 4, 2011 (Washington, DC). http://www.fpif.org/articles/interview_with_phyllis_bennis.

13. Robert Littwak, *Rogue States and U.S. Foreign Policy* (Washington, DC: Woodrow Wilson Center Press, 2000), 8. See also Michael Klare, *Rogue States and Nuclear Outlaws* (New York: Hill and Wang, 1996).

14. According to a 1995 Program on International Policy Attitudes poll, 89 percent of Americans preferred working through the UN on the use of military force and only 29 percent preferred going it alone. Cited in Bradley Podliska, *Acting Alone* (Lanham, MD: Lexington Books, 2010), 15.

15. William Kristol and Robert Kagan, "Toward a Neo-Reaganite Foreign Policy," *Foreign Affairs*, July/August 1996, http://www.carnegieendowment.org/publications/index.cfm?fa=view&id=276.

16. Fawaz Gerges points out that although Osama bin Laden created al-Qaeda in 1988, the organization didn't become truly operational in any meaningful sense until the second half of the 1990s. Fawaz Gerges, *The*

Rise and Fall of Al-Qaeda (New York: Oxford University Press, 2011), 29. Qutb, although he advocated violence, did not advise attacking the United States.

17. The United States operated the Dhahran airfield in Saudi Arabia from 1945 to 1962, but U.S. military presence in the country only became a major point of friction around the time of the first Gulf War.

18. Bernard Lewis, "The Roots of Muslim Rage," *Atlantic*, September 1990, http://www.theatlantic.com/magazine/archive/1990/09/the-roots-of-muslim-rage/4643/.

19. Daniel Pipes, "The Muslims Are Coming, The Muslims Are Coming," *National Interest*, November 19, 1990, http://www.danielpipes.org/198/the-muslims-are-coming-the-muslims-are-coming.

20. Quoted in Daniel Pipes, *Militant Islam Reaches America*, 95.

21. "Fundamentalist Menace," *Times*, June 10, 1990.

22. Elaine Scioliono, "Seeing Green," *New York Times Magazine*, Janaury 21, 1996, http://query.nytimes.com/gst/fullpage.html?res=9C06E1D81339F932A15752C0A960958260&sec=&spon=&pagewanted=all.

23. Daniel Pipes, *Militant Islam Reaches America*, 245.

24. Elaine Scioliono, "Seeing Green," *New York Times Magazine*, Janaury 21, 1996.

25. Samuel Huntington, "The Clash of Civilizations," *Foreign Affairs*, Summer 1993.

26. Norman Podhoretz, *World War IV* (New York: Doubleday, 2007), 9.

27. David Frum, *The Right Man* (New York: Random House, 2005), 235–36.

28. "Bush: Islamic Radicalism Doomed To Fail," CNN, October 6, 2005, http://edition.cnn.com/2005/POLITICS/10/06/bush.transcript/.

29. See, most recently, Jeffrey Herf, *Nazi Propaganda for the Arab World* (New Haven, CT: Yale University Press, 2009).

30. Malise Ruthven, "Faith and Reason: Construing Islam as a Language," *Independent*, September 8, 1990; the more contemporary use of the term with its neoconservative spin probably began with Khalid Duran, a Muslim scholar from Germany, in a July 20, 2001, interview with *Washington Times*. See "Islamofascism By Any Other Name," *Washington Times*, September 1, 2006, http://www.washingtontimes.com/news/2006/sep/1/20060901-090752-7525r/.

31. Elaine Scioliono, "Seeing Green," *New York Times Magazine*, Janaury 21, 1996.

32. According to the gloss that early neoconservative Jeanne Kirkpatrick provided in her book *Dictatorships and Double Standards*, the West had every reason to support right-wing authoritarian dictatorships because they would steadfastly oppose left-wing totalitarian dictatorships, which,

unlike the autocracies we allied with, were supposedly incapable of internal reform. Jeanne Kirkpatrick, *Dictatorships and Double Standards* (New York: Simon and Schuster, 1982).

33. Bassam Tibi, "The Totalitarianism of Jihadist Islam and Its Challenge to Europe and Islam," in *Totalitarian Movements and Political Religions* 8, no. 1, March 2007. On Islamist vanguardism, also see Thomas Friedman, *The World Is Flat* (New York: Farrar, Straus, and Giroux, 2007), 558.

34. This discourse on Islamofascism had more than a whiff of the earlier Marxist and post-Marxist discussions of "Oriental despotism" and "Asiatic modes of production."

35. Podhoretz, *World War IV*, 217.

36. Ibid., p. 14; or, as terrorism pundit Steven Emerson puts it in one of the most popular books on terrorism that came out just after 9/11, "This is the most important battle of our time." Steven Emerson, *American Jihad* (New York: Free Press, 2002), 25

37. Daniel Pipes, *Militant Islam Reaches America*, 89. Others, like former assistant secretary of state for human rights and humanitarian affairs Richard Schifter, expanded this third "totalitarian" threat facing the United States to embrace "an informal *de facto* alliance of neo-fascists and neo-communists, an alliance that unites Mahmoud Akhmadinejad with Hugo Chavez." Richard Schifter, "The Clash of Ideologies," http://www.jewishlawyers.org/media/user/documents/Schifter_keynote_address_04-20-2009.pdf.

38. Michael Ignatieff, *Empire Lite* (New York: Vintage, 2003).

39. Peter Beinart, *The Good Fight* (New York: Harper Collins, 2006), xii.

40. Beinart doesn't make the mistake of some of the conservative opponents of "Islamofascism," for he distinguishes between different types of political Islam.

41. Beinart, *The Good Fight*, 194.

42. Paul Berman, *Terror and Liberalism* (New York: Norton, 2003), 4, 13.

43. Other *jihad* liberals have followed Berman's lead. "Like fundamentalist Judaism and Medieval Christianity, Islam is totalist," writes Martin Amis. "That is to say, it makes a total claim on the individual." Here Amis qualifies Judaism and Christianity—only versions of the religion are totalitarian—but reserves his judgment on Islam to the entire religion. Martin Amis, *The Second Plane*, 77.

44. Paul Berman, *The Flight of the Intellectuals* (New York: Melville House, 2010), 201. For a careful dissection of Berman's errors, see Malise Ruthven, "Righteous and Wrong," *New York Review of Books*, August 19, 2010.

45. Ibid., 155.

46. Stephan Salisbury, *Mohamed's Ghosts* (New York: Nation Books, 2010), 6.

47. Arun Kundnani, "Islamism and the Roots of Liberal Rage," *Race and Class*, October 2008, 52.

48. Sam Harris, "Head-in-the-Sand Liberals," *Los Angeles Times*, September 18, 2006, http://www.samharris.org/site/full_text/the-end-of-liberalism/.

49. "Richard Dawkins on Islam," September 26, 2010, http://www.faithfreedom.org/videos-features/richard-dawkins-on-islam/.

50. Yolande Knell, "Jordan's Democracy on Show," BBC News, November 8, 2010, http://www.bbc.co.uk/news/world-middle-east-11702306.

51. Noah Feldman, *After Jihad* (New York: Farrar, Straus, and Giroux, 1993), 3–5.

52. Edward Djerejian, *Danger and Opportunity* (New York: Simon and Schuster, 2008), 22.

53. Anthropologist Claude Levi-Strauss provides another example. As he wrote in *Tristes Tropiques*, Islam is intolerant and hermetic, based on "an inability to establish links with the outside world." Claude Levi-Strauss, *Tristes Tropiques* (New York: Washington Square Press, 1977), 460.

54. Philip Howard, *The Digital Origins of Dictatorship and Democracy* (New York: Oxford University Press, 2010), 37.

55. Quoted in, "Hamas." Council on Foreign Relations, http://www.cfr.org/israel/hamas/p8968#p6.

56. Quoted in Reese Erlich, *Conversations with Terrorists* (PoliPoint Press, 2010), 44.

57. Robert Leiken and Steven Brooke, "The Moderate Muslim Brotherhood," *Foreign Affairs*, March/April 2007, 108.

58. Lorenzo Vidino, *The New Muslim Brotherhood in the West* (New York: Columbia University Press, 2010), 59.

59. Ibid., 111.

60. Ibid., 219.

61. Alistair Crooke, *Resistance* (London: Pluto, 2009), 81.

62. Netherlands Scientific Council for Government Policy, *Dynamism in Islamic Activism* (Amsterdam: Amsterdam University Press, 2006), 37.

63. Interview with John Esposito, January 21, 2011 (by phone), http://www.fpif.org/articles/interview_with_john_esposito.

64. "Islamic Calvinists," European Stability Initiative, September 19, 2005, http://www.esiweb.org/index.php?lang=en&id=156&document_ID=69.

65. Robert Worth, "Preaching Moderate Islam and Becoming a TV Star," *New York Times*, January 2, 2009, http://www.nytimes.com/2009/01/03/world/middleeast/03preacher.html?_r=1&pagewanted=all; Aa Gym's

popularity plummeted when he took a second wife in 2006, but he continues to try to rebuild his following. See James B Hoesterey, "Aa Gym," *Inside Indonesia*, October/November 2007, http://www.insideindonesia.org/edition-90/aa-gym.

66. "Between 2000 and 2010, the compound annual growth rate of internet users was 32 percent, compared with 24 percent for the rest of the developing world," Philip Howard, *The Digital Origins of Dictatorship and Democracy*, 32, 37.

67. Noah Feldman, *After Jihad*, 8.

68. Fred Kaplan, "The Professional," *New York Times Magazine*, February 10, 2008, http://www.nytimes.com/2008/02/10/magazine/10gates-t.html?_r=2&pagewanted=all.

69. I explored these dynamics in John Feffer, *Beyond Détente* (New York: Noonday Press, 1990),116–29.

Chapter Three

1. Peter Ford, "Europe Cringes at Bush 'Crusade' against Terrorists," *Christian Science Monitor*, September 19, 2010, http://www.csmonitor.com/2001/0919/p12s2-woeu.html.

2. "Jihad against Jews and Crusaders," *World Islamic Front*, February 23, 1998, http://www.fas.org/irp/world/para/docs/980223-fatwa.htm.

3. "President Rallies the Troops in Alaska," White House, February 16, 2002, http://georgewbush-whitehouse.archives.gov/news/releases/2002/02/20020216-1.html.

4. "Pentagon to Change Operation's Code Name," *Mercury News*, September 20, 2001, http://wwrn.org/articles/5019/.

5. "Transcript of President Bush's Address," CNN, September 21, 2001, http://articles.cnn.com/2001-09-20/us/gen.bush.transcript_1_joint-session-national-anthem-citizens/2?_s=PM:US.

6. After the retaliatory air strikes in Sudan and Afghanistan following the 1998 embassy bombings, President Clinton "went out of his way to distinguish between Islam and terrorism, between the faith of Muslims and its distortion by those who committed acts of terrorism in the name of Islam." John Esposito, *The Islamic Threat* (New York: Oxford University Press, 1999), 277.

7. Janelle Brown, "Anti-Arab Passions Sweep the U.S." Salon, September 13, 2001, http://www.salon.com/news/feature/2001/09/13/backlash.

8. Dana Milbank and Emily Wax, "Bush Visits Mosque to Forestall Hate Crimes," *Washington Post*, September 18, 2001, http://www.washingtonpost.com/ac2/wp-dyn?pagename=article&node=nation/specials/attacked&contentId=A46832-2001Sep17&notFound=true.

9. Balbir Singh Sodi in Mesa, Arizona, on September 15, 2001; Waqar Hasan in Dallas, Texas, on September 15, 2001; Adel Karas in San Gabriel, California, on September 15, 2001; Ali Almansoop in Detroit, Michigan, on September 21, 2001; and Vasudev Patel in Mesquite, Texas, on October 4, 2001. See Nadine Naber, "Look, Mohammed, the Terrorist is Coming" in Amaney Jamal and Nadine Naber, eds. *Race and Arab-Americans after 9/11* (Syracuse, NY: Syracuse University Press, 2008), 289.

10. "Bush Criticizes Attacks on Arab-Americans," ABC News, September 17, 2001, http://abcnews.go.com/US/story?id=92486&page=1.

11. Anny Bakalian and Mehdi Bozorgmehr, *Backlash 9/11* (Berkeley: University of California Press, 2009), 173.

12. Ibid., 181.

13. R.S. Zaharna, *Battles to Bridges* (New York: Palgrave MacMillan, 2010), 30.

14. Some, like Reuel Marc Gerecht, advised U.S. policy makers to make their peace with Islamists. "Many Israelis and their American supporters may rise in horror contemplating replacing peace-treaty-signing dictators with fundamentalists who may partly build a democratic consensus on anti-Zionism. But down this uneasy path lies an end to bin Ladenism and the specter of an American city attacked with weapons of mass destruction," Gerecht writes in *The Islamic Paradox* (Washington, DC: American Enterprise Institute Press, 2004), 58.

15. Lorenzo Vidino, *The New Muslim Brotherhood in the West*, 6.

16. Akhbar Ahmed, *Journey into America* (Washington, DC: Brookings Institution, 2010), 435.

17. At the end of his first voyage, Columbus wrote that his purpose was "to conquer the world, spread the Christian faith, and regain the Holy Land and the Temple Mount." Fuad Sha'ban, *For Zion's Sake* (London: Pluto, 2005), 22. His arch-rival Vasco de Gama also launched his voyages of discovery, in the opposite direction toward Indian Ocean, to defeat Islam as well by uniting Christians east and west. See Nigel Cliff, *Holy War* (New York: Harper Collins, 2011).

18. Ibid., 79–80.

19. Robert Kagan, *Dangerous Nation* (New York: Knopf, 2006).

20. Richard Leiby, "Terrorists by Another Name," *Washington Post*, October 15, 2001, http://www.washingtonpost.com/ac2/wp-dyn/A59720-2001Oct14?language=printer.

21. Thomas Jewett, "Terrorism in Early America," *Early America Review*, Winter/Spring 2002, http://www.earlyamerica.com/review/2002_winter_spring/terrorism.htm, Joshua London, "America's Earliest Terrorists,"

National Review, December 16, 2005, http://www.nationalreview.com/comment/london200512160955.asp; Forcier quoted in Frank Lambert, *The Barbary Wars*, 8.

22. Frank Lambert, *The Barbary Wars* (New York: Hill and Wang, 2005).

23. Michael Kitzen, *Tripoli and the United States at War* (Jefferson, NC: McFarland, 1993).

24. The president did mention the pirates in reference to general Mideast policy, however. See, for example, "President George W. Bush's Remarks to the Saban Forum," *Haaretz*, December 8, 2006, http://www.haaretz.com/news/president-george-w-bush-s-remarks-to-the-saban-forum-1.258930.

25. Malcolm Gladwell, *Blink* (New York: Little, Brown, 2005).

26. Hamish McDonald, "Cheney's Tough Talking Derails Negotiations with North Korea," *Sydney Morning Herald*, December 22, 2003.

27. See John Lewis Gaddis, *Strategies of Containment* (New York: Oxford University Press, 1982), 89ff.

28. R. S. Zaharna, *Battles to Bridges*, 12.

29. Imam Feisal Abudl Rauf, *What's Right with Islam* (HarperSanFrancisco, 2004), 162.

30. For instance: "The OIC is the collective voice of the Muslim world. It has always stood against and expressed condemnation of violence, extremism and terrorism perpetrated in the name of Islam." "Combating Extremists," *OIC Journal*, September–December 2009, 3.

31. For CAIR's statement and a compilation of similar statements from other Muslim organizations, see CAIR's Anti-Terrorism Campaigns, http://www.cair.com/AmericanMuslims/AntiTerrorism.aspx.

32. Fawaz Gerges, *The Rise and Fall of Al-Qaeda*, 14.

33. "Osama bin Laden Largely Discredited among Muslim Publics in Recent Years," Pew Research Center, May 2, 2011, http://www.pewglobal.org/2011/05/02/osama-bin-laden-largely-discredited-among-muslim-publics-in-recent-years/.

34. R. S. Zaharna, *Battles to Bridges*, 44.

35. Craig Whitlock, "U.S. Network Falters in Mideast Mission," *Washington Post*, June 23, 2008, http://www.washingtonpost.com/wp-dyn/content/article/2008/06/22/AR2008062201228.html.

36. Sayyid Qutb, for instance, was appalled at what he saw during his two-year stay in the United States in the 1940s, and that was pretty tame by today's standards.

37. David Cole, "Are We Safer?," *New York Review of Books*, March 9, 2006.

38. Stephan Salisbury, *Mohamed's Ghosts* (New York: Nation Books, 2010), 21.

39. Michael Bohn, *The Achille Lauro Hijacking* (Dulles, VA: Brassey's, 2004), 35–38.

40. Greg Krikorian, "Evidence Emerges in '85 Santa Ana Slaying," *Los Angeles Times*, October 11, 2007, http://articles.latimes.com/2007/oct/11/local/me-odeh11; for JDL statement, see "Backgrounder: Jewish Defense League," http://www.adl.org/extremism/jdl_chron.asp.

41. "Jewish Defense League Leader Declared Brain Dead in Suicide," *New York Times*, November 5, 2002, http://select.nytimes.com/gst/abstract.html?res=FA0C1FF9395A0C768CDDA80994DA404482.

42. See "We Are Not the Enemy", *Human Rights Watch*, 14, no. 6 (November 2002), 11.

43. Edward Curtis, *Muslims in America* (New York: Oxford University Press, 2009), 29. Curtis also points out that there was a flip side as well: "it was also increasingly understood as romantic, adventurous, and, for religious liberals . . . innately spiritual."

44. Jack Shaheen, *Reel Bad Arabs* (New York: Olive Branch Press, 2001), 16.

45. Quoted in David Lam, "Loyalty Questioned," *Los Angeles Times*, March 13, 1987, http://articles.latimes.com/print/1987-03-13/news/mn-5585_1_arab-identity.

46. Louise Cainkar, *Homeland Insecurity* (New York: Russell Sage Foundation, 2009), 88.

47. Anthony Toth, "On Arabs and Islam," *Washington Report on Middle Eastern Affairs*, January 1987, http://wrmea.com/backissues/0187/87010012.html.

48. Farhan Haq, "Anti-Muslim Crimes Higher than Gulf War Period," Inter Press Service, May 24, 1995.

49. Louise Cainkar, *Homeland Insecurity*, 69. In 1993, after the World Trade Center bombing, a Gallup poll found that 32% of Americans had an unfavorable opinion about Arabs. Jeffrey Jones, "Americans Felt Uneasy toward Arabs Even Before September 11," Gallup News Service, September 28, 2001. http://www.gallup.com/poll/4939/Americans-Felt-Uneasy-Toward-Arabs-Even-Before-September.aspx.

50. Susan Akram and Kevin R. Johnson, "Race and Civil Rights pre-September 11, 2001," in Elaine Hagopian, ed. *Civil Rights in Peril* (Chicago: Haymarket Books, 2004), 13, 21.

51. *We Are Not the Enemy*, Human Rights Watch, 17.

52. Federal Bureau of Investigation, "Hate Crime Statistics, 2001," http://www.fbi.gov/about-us/cjis/ucr/hate-crime/2001.

53. *We Are Not the Enemy*, Human Rights Watch, 17.

54. Stephan Salisbury, *Mohamed's Ghosts*, 104.

55. Paul Vitello, "In Fierce Opposition to a Muslim Center, Echoes of an Old Fight," *New York Times*, October 8, 2010, A19.

56. Louise Cainkar, *Homeland Insecurity*, 237.

57. According to the FBI's hate-crime statistics for 2008, anti-Jewish hate crimes accounted for 69 percent of all religiously motivated crimes, compared to 7.5 percent for anti-Muslim crimes, http://www.fbi.gov/about-us/cjis/ucr/hate-crime/2008.

58. "Imus Anchor on Palestinians: 'Stinking animals. They ought to drop the bomb right there, kill 'em all right now.'" *Media Matters*, November 19, 2004, http://mediamatters.org/research/200411190009.

Chapter Four

1. "Obama's Speech at AIPAC," NPR, June 4, 2008, http://www.npr.org/templates/story/story.php?storyId=91150432.

2. "McCain Repudiates 'Hussein Obama' Remarks," *Caucus*, February 26, 2008, http://thecaucus.blogs.nytimes.com/2008/02/26/mccain-repudiates-hussein-obama-remarks/.

3. Alex Koppelman, "Why the Stories about Obama's Birth Certificate Will Never Die," *Salon*, December 5, 2008, http://www.salon.com/news/feature/2008/12/05/birth_certificate/.

4. Jim Kuhnhen, "Obama Photo in Turban, Robe Causes Stir," *Huffington Post*, February 25, 2008, http://www.huffingtonpost.com/2008/02/25/obama-photo-in-turban-rob_n_88272.html.

5. "Obama's Nation of Islam Staffers, Edward Said & 'Inflexible Jews' Causing Mid-East Conflict: An Obama Insider Reveals the Real Barack," January 30, 2008, http://www.debbieschlussel.com/3356/exclusive-obamas-nation-of-islam-staffers-edward-said-inflexible-jews-causing-mid-east-conflict-an-obama-insider-reveals-the-real-barack/.

6. James Zogby, "It's a Damn Shame," *Huffington Post*, August 8, 2008, http://www.huffingtonpost.com/james-zogby/its-a-damn-shame_b_117839.html; Esposito, 20.

7. Karen Armstrong, *Holy War*, 418–19.

8. "A Third of Public, Including Three in Five Republicans, Support the Tea Party Movement and About a Quarter Oppose It," Harris Poll, March 31, 2010, http://www.harrisinteractive.com/vault/Harris_Interactive_Poll_Tea_Party_Opposition_2010_03.pdf.

9. Audrey Gillan, "Obama Would Welcome Talks with Taliban Moderates," *Guardian*, March 8, 2009, http://www.guardian.co.uk/world/2009/mar/08/barack-obama-talks-taliban-afghanistan.

10. "National Security Strategy," White House, May 2010, 4, http://www.

whitehouse.gov/sites/default/files/rss_viewer/national_security_strategy.
pdf.

11. Mitchell Bard, *The Arab Lobby* (New York: Harper Collins, 2010), x.

12. Tim Wildmon, "Obama Gives Your Tax Dollars to Rebuild Muslim
Mosques around the World," *Canada Free Press*, August 26, 2010, http://
canadafreepress.com/index.php/article/26990.

13. Frank Gaffney, "America's First Muslim President?" *Washington Times*,
June 9, 2009, http://www.washingtontimes.com/news/2009/jun/09/
americas-first-muslim-president/.

14. "Remarks by the President on a New Beginning," White House,
June 4, 2009. http://www.whitehouse.gov/the_press_office/
Remarks-by-the-President-at-Cairo-University-6-04-09/.

15. Greg Miller, "CIA Steps up Drone Attacks in Pakistan amid Fear of
Al-Qaeda Terror in Europe," *Washington Post*, September 29, 2010.
http://www.washingtonpost.com/wp-dyn/content/article/2010/09/28/
AR2010092806841.html.

16. Philip Alston, "Report of the Special Rapporteur on Extrajudicial,
Summary or Arbitrary Executions," UN General Assembly, Human
Rights Council, May 28, 2010, 25, http://www2.ohchr.org/english/
bodies/hrcouncil/docs/14session/A.HRC.14.24.Add6.pdf.

17. Charlie Savage, "UN Report Highly Critical of US Drone Attacks,"
New York Times, June 2, 2010, http://www.nytimes.com/2010/06/03/
world/03drones.html.

18. Spencer Ackerman, "'Unprecedented' Drone Assault," *Wired*,
December 17, 2010, http://www.wired.com/dangerroom/2010/12/
unprecedented-drone-strikes-hit-pakistan-in-late-2010/.

19. "The Year of the Drone," New America Foundation, http://
counterterrorism.newamerica.net/drones.

20. Karen De Young and Greg Jaffe, "U.S. 'Secret War' Expands Globally
as Special Operations Forces Take Larger Role," *Washington Post*,
June 4, 2010, http://www.washingtonpost.com/wp-dyn/content/
article/2010/06/03/AR2010060304965.html.

21. Here is the polling to support this composite picture of Egyptian
public opinion. According to Pew Global Attitudes Project, only 18
percent of Egyptians support U.S. anti-terror efforts and only 15
percent believe that U.S. troops should stay in Afghanistan. Also, only
20 percent had favorable views about Osama bin Laden, and only 20
percent support suicide bombings. "Obama More Popular Abroad Than
at Home, Global Image of U.S. Continues to Benefit," Pew Global
Attitudes Project, June 17, 2010, http://pewglobal.org/2010/06/17/
obama-more-popular-abroad-than-at-home/.

22. Ibid.
23. Aamer Madhani, "Is Obama's Outreach to Muslims Working?," *National Journal*, November 9, 2010, http://nationaljournal.com/whitehouse/is-obama-s-outreach-to-muslims-working—20101109.
24. Juan Cole, *Engaging the Muslim World*, 237.
25. Robert Pape, "What Triggers the Suicide Bomber?" *Los Angeles Times*, October 22, 2010, http://articles.latimes.com/2010/oct/22/opinion/la-oe-pape-fgn-occupation-20101022.
26. M. Junaid Levesque-Alam, "Robert Wright and the Koran," *Foreign Policy in Focus*, September 15, 2010, http://www.fpif.org/blog/robert_wright_and_the_Qur'an_grappling_with_the_wrong_religion.
27. Steven Kull, "Muslims and America: Internalizing the Clash of Civilizations," *World Public Opinion*, June 7, 2010, http://www.worldpublicopinion.org/pipa/articles/brmiddleeastnafricara/663.php?nid=&id=&pnt=663&lb=.
28. According to Gallup polling, substantial majorities in nearly all nations surveyed (95% in Burkina Faso, 94% in Egypt, 93% in Iran, and 90% in Indonesia) would guarantee freedom of speech if drafting a constitution. Equally substantial majorities said that women should have same legal rights as men: 85% in Iran, 90% range in Indonesia, Bangladesh, Turkey and Lebanon; 77% in Pakistan; 61% in Saudi Arabia. John Esposito and Dalia Mogahed, *Who Speaks for Islam?* 47, 51.
29. Jamie Novogrod, "Bachmann Condemns Arab Spring, Blames It on Obama," MSNBC, September 29, 2011, http://firstread.msnbc.msn.com/_news/2011/09/29/8038856-bachmann-condemns-arab-spring-blames-it-on-obama.
30. "Islam and Democracy: Uneasy Companions," *Economist*, August 6, 2011, http://www.economist.com/node/21525410.
31. Ray Takeyh, " U.S. Must Take Sides to Keep the Arab Spring from Islamist Takeover," *Washington Post*, March 23, 2011, http://www.washingtonpost.com/opinions/us-must-take-sides-to-keep-the-arab-spring-from-islamist-takeover/2011/03/23/ABNhI2KB_story.html.
32. As a former CIA officer writes: "Al-Qaeda's leaders, Osama bin Laden and Ayman Zawahiri, started their political lives affiliated with the Brotherhood, but both have denounced it for decades as too soft and a cat's paw of Mubarak and America." Bruce Reidel, "Don't Fear Egypt's Muslim Brotherhood," *Daily Beast*, January 27, 2011, http://www.thedailybeast.com/articles/2011/01/27/muslim-brotherhood-could-win-in-egypt-protests-and-why-obama-shouldnt-worry.html.
33. On the left, see Robert Dreyfuss, "Three Questions on Obama's Great Libyan Adventure," *Nation*, August 31, 2011, http://www.thenation.

com/blog/163070/three-questions-obamas-great-libyan-adventure; on the right, see Bill Gertz, "Jihadists Plot to Take Over Libya," *Washington Times*, September 4, 2011. http://www.washingtontimes.com/news/2011/sep/4/jihadists-plot-to-take-over-libya/?page=all; and for a *Daily Show* clip featuring Jon Stewart, see Paul Woodward, "Islamophobia—On the Daily Show," *War in Context*, April 5, 2011, http://warincontext.org/2011/04/05/islamophobia-on-the-daily-show/.

34. Charles Levinson, "Ex-Mujahedeen Help Lead Libyan Rebels," *Wall Street Journal*, April 3, 2011, http://online.wsj.com/article/SB100014240527487037312504576237042432212406.html.

35. Rod Nordland, "Senior American Diplomat in Tripoli Says Islamists Are Not a Threat," *New York Times*, September 14, 2011, http://www.nytimes.com/2011/09/15/world/africa/senior-american-diplomat-in-tripoli-says-islamists-are-not-a-threat.html; Abigail Hauslohner, "Libya's Revolution Produces a New Hybrid: Pro-Western Islamists," *Time*, September 16, 2011, http://www.time.com/time/world/article/0,8599,2093518,00.html.

36. Corey Flintoff, "What Role Will Islamists Play in Libya?" *National Public Radio*, September 21, 2011, http://www.npr.org/2011/09/21/140665324/what-role-will-islamists-play-in-libya.

37. Amitabh Pal, *"Islam" Means Peace*. Although violent movements eventually emerged in both Kosovo and the Occupied Territories, the nonviolent efforts were much more popular, broad-based, and, in many ways, successful.

38. Islamophobes in the United States often argue that the Muslim Brotherhood controls all major U.S. Muslim organizations as part of its clandestine mission to establish a global caliphate. They point to a single memo written by a Brotherhood member that came to light in a legal case against a Muslim American organization. "Nobody has ever produced any evidence that the document was more than something produced by the daydream of one enthusiast," says Nathan Brown, professor of political science and international affairs, and director of the Institute for Middle East Studies at the George Washington University. Sarah Posner, "Welcome to the Shari'ah Conspiracy Theory Industry," *Religious Dispatches*, March 8, 2011, http://www.religiondispatches.org/archive/politics/4335/welcome_to_the_shari'ah_conspiracy_theory_industry/.

39. Peter Mansfield, *The Arabs* (London: Penguin, 1985), 507.

40. For the answer to the survey question, see http://abcnews.go.com/images/politics/obama1_1.pdf; for the 2006 speech, see Barack Obama, "Floor Statement of Senator Barack Obama: PATRIOT Act

Reauthorization," February 16, 2006, http://obamaspeeches.com/053-Floor-Statement-S2271-PATRIOT-Act-Reauthorization-Obama-Speech.htm.

41. Michael Farrell, "Obama Signs Patriot Act Extension without Reforms," *Christian Science Monitor*, March 1, 2010, http://www.csmonitor.com/USA/Politics/2010/0301/Obama-signs-Patriot-Act-extension-without-reforms.

42. Eric Schmitt and Charlie Savage, "In U.S. Sting Operations, Questions of Entrapment," *New York Times*, November 29, 2010, http://www.nytimes.com/2010/11/30/us/politics/30fbi.html?ref=mohamed_osman_mohamud.

43. Richard Bernstein, "A Defense That Could Be Obsolete," *New York Times*, December 1, 2010, http://www.nytimes.com/2010/12/02/us/02iht-letter.html?_r=1&ref=richard_bernstein.

44. Ted Conover, "The Pathetic Newburgh Four," *Slate*, November 23, 2010, http://www.slate.com/id/2275735/.

45. Stephan Salisbury, "Plotting Terrorism," *TomDispatch*, July 6, 2010, http://www.tomdispatch.com/post/175270/tomgram:_stephan_salisbury,_plotting_terrorism__/.

46. Stephan Salisbury, *Mohamed's Ghosts*, 182.

47. Ibid.

48. Jerry Markon, "Tension Grows between Calif. Muslims, FBI after Informant Infiltrates Mosque," *Washington Post*, December 5, 2010, http://www.washingtonpost.com/wp-dyn/content/article/2010/12/04/AR2010120403710_pf.html.

49. Kelley Vlahos, "Tensions between FBI and Muslims over Entrapment Charges Growing," *Change.org*, December 7, 2010, http://criminaljustice.change.org/blog/view/tensions_between_fbi_and_muslims_over_entrapment_charges_growing.

50. David Schanzer, Charles Kurzman, and Ebrahim Moosa, "Anti-Terror Lessons of Muslim-Americans," January 6, 2010, 22. http://www.sanford.duke.edu/news/Schanzer_Kurzman_Moosa_Anti-Terror_Lessons.pdf.

51. Arun Kundnani, "The FBI's 'Good' Muslims," *Nation*, September 19, 2011, 20.

52. "One Year After Obama's Cairo Speech, U.S. Policies Continue To Unfairly Target Muslims," ACLU, June 4, 2010, http://www.aclu.org/human-rights-national-security/one-year-after-obamas-cairo-speech-us-policies-continue-unfairly-targ.

53. Quoted in "What Counts as Abetting Terrorists," *New York Times*, June 21, 2010, http://roomfordebate.blogs.nytimes.com/2010/06/21/what-counts-as-abetting-terrorists/.

54. Another danger is the application of this profiling to other communities. In fall 2010, the Justice Department began to crack down on antiwar activists because of their alleged connections to terrorist organizations abroad. In September, FBI agents raided homes and offices of activists and issued subpoenas to 14 people, including those connected to the Minneapolis-based Women Against Military Madness, the Chicago-based Arab American Action Network, and Students for a Democratic Society. See Jeremy Gantz, "Terrorist by Association," *In These Times*, December 13, 2010, http://inthesetimes.com/article/6745/terrorist_by_association.

55. This data also includes the Beltway snipers who killed eleven people, which is questionable, since it straddled the line between serial murder and terrorism. Charles Kurzman, David Schanzer, and Ebrahim Moosa, "Muslim American Terrorism Since 9/11:Why So Rare?" *Muslim World*, 2011, 467, http://sanford.duke.edu/centers/tcths/documents/Kurzman_Schanzer_Moosa_Muslim_American_Terrorism.pdf.

56. Ibid.

57. Ibid., 483.

58. David Brock, *Blinded by the Right* (New York: Crown, 2002).

59. This network, in place well before the Park51 controversy, includes David Horowitz and his Freedom Center, Daniel Pipes and his Middle East Forum, the Washington Institute for Near East Policy and the Middle East Media Research Institute, as well as the multi-issue conservative outfits such as the Heritage Foundation, the American Enterprise Institute, and the Hudson Institute. For more details on the foundations, institutions, and individuals behind this network, see Wajahat Ali et al., *Fear, Inc.*

60. Max Blumenthal, "The Great Fear," *TomDispatch*, December 19, 2010, http://www.tomdispatch.com/blog/175334/.

61. "Public Islamic School Most Violent in NY: Everyday Terror at Intifada High School," *Atlas Shrugs*, March 19, 2010, http://atlasshrugs2000.typepad.com/atlas_shrugs/khalil_gibran_international_academy/.

62. Jennifer Medina, "Ex-Principal of Arabic School Won't Sue City," *New York Times*, May 25, 2010. http://www.nytimes.com/2010/05/26/nyregion/26principal.html?_r=1&emc=eta1.

63. Dana Sauchelli and Gersh Kuntzman, "Fatwa! City Will Kill Gibran Middle School Due to Poor Numbers, Performance," *Brooklyn*

Paper, April 6, 2011, http://brooklynpaper.com/stories/34/14/
dtg_gibrandead_2011_4_8_bk.html.

64. Daniel Pipes, "A Madrassah Grows in Brooklyn," *New York Sun*, April 24,
2007, http://www.danielpipes.org/4441/a-madrasa-grows-in-brooklyn.

65. Pamela Geller, "Bin Laden/Al Qaeda Funding Ground Zero Mosque
Imam Rauf," Atlasshrugs.com, July 31, 2010, http://atlasshrugs2000.
typepad.com/atlas_shrugs/2010/07/terror-finded-ground-zero-
mosque-imam-raufs-bin-laden-link.html; Kenneth Vogel and Giovanni
Russonello, "Latest Mosque Issue: The Money Trail," *Politico*, September
5, 2010, http://www.politico.com/news/stories/0910/41767.html.

66. "Fox Provides Megaphone to NYC Mosque Opponents," *Media Matters*,
August 13, 2010, http://mediamatters.org/research/201008130015.

67. Imam Feisal Abdul Rauf, *What's Right with Islam* (HarperSanFrancisco,
2004), 6. On Hamas, see Lisa Miller, "Feisal Abdul Rauf," *Newsweek*,
December 23, 2010, http://www.newsweek.com/2010/12/23/feisal-
abdul-rauf.html.

68. U.S. Department of State, "Daily Press Briefing," August 10, 2010,
http://www.state.gov/r/pa/prs/dpb/2010/08/145853.htm.

69. Laurie Goodstein, "Across Nation, Mosque Projects Meet Opposition,"
New York Times, August 7, 2010, http://www.nytimes.com/2010/08/08/
us/08mosque.html.

70. Edward Curtis, "Five Myths about Mosques in America," *Washington
Post*, August 29, 2010, http://www.washingtonpost.com/wp-dyn/content/
article/2010/08/26/AR2010082605510.html. What sociologists interpret
as integration into society—such as the greater public engagement of
Muslims—is perceived as just the opposite by politicians and the public
out of ignorance or because of well-funded media manipulation. Neil
MacMaster, "Islamophobia in France and the 'Algerian Problem,'"
in Emran Qureshi and Michael Sells, *The New Crusades* (New York:
Columbia University Press, 2003), 297.

71. Gaffney's animus toward Muslims goes back much further. In 2003,
he conducted smear campaigns against several Muslim staffers in the
George W. Bush White House. See Wajahat Ali et al., *Fear, Inc.* 35–36.

72. *Shariah: The Threat to America*, (*Center for Security Policy*, 2010), 5–6.

73. Feldman, *The Fall and Rise of the Islamic State* (Princeton: Princeton
University Press, 2008), 115.

74. Ibid., 11.

75. Michaelangelo Conte, "State Court Throws Out Religion as Defense,"
Jersey Journal, August 2, 2010, http://www.nj.com/news/jjournal/index.
ssf?/base/news-5/1280731209222240.xml&coll=3.

76. A second case, cited by actor Chuck Norris in an anti-sharia article, concerns a judge ruling in Florida that a contract dispute between Muslim parties would "proceed under Ecclesiastical Islamic Law." But as Adam Jacobson of Human Rights First remarks, "in cases where an agreement drawn up according to religious law is disputed, religious law can be used to arbitrate a decision. The supposed 'far-reaching' implications of this case and the legal application of Sharia law end there." Adam Jacobson, "Chuck Norris and the Fake Threat of a Sharia Invasion," *Human Rights First*, April 21, 2011, http://www.humanrightsfirst.org/2011/04/21/. chuck-norris-and-the-fake-threat-of-a-sharia-invasion/

77. Tim Lockette, "Legislation Would Ban Islamic Law in Alabama Courts," *Anniston Star*, March 4, 2011, http://www.annistonstar.com/pages/full_story/push?article-Legislation+would+ban+Islamic+law+in+Alabama+courts-%20&id=1215 7691&instance=recentComments.

78. John Feffer, "Interview with Wajahat Ali," *Foreign Policy in Focus*, March 11, 2011, http://www.fpif.org/articles/interview_with_wajahat_ali.

79. Ed Brayton, "Controversial Experts Authored 'Shariah' Report Hailed by Bachmann," *Minnesota Independent*, September 22, 2010, http://minnesotaindependent.com/70974/ controversial-experts-authored-shariah-report-hailed-by-bachmann.

80. Dana Priest and William Arkin, "Monitoring America," *Washington Post*, December 20, 2010.

81. Ibid.

82. "Liddy Guest Walid Shoebat Falsely Claimed That Obama Is 'Definitely a Muslim,'" *Media Matters*, September 11, 2008, http://mediamatters. org/research/200809110018; Omar Sacirbey, "Skeptics Challenge Life Stories Offered by High-profile Muslim Converts to Christianity," *The Washington Post*, June 26, 2010. http://www.washingtonpost.com/wp-dyn/content/article/2010/06/25/AR2010062504435.html.

83. Jorg Luyken, "The Palestinian 'Terrorist' Turned Zionist," *Jerusalem Post*, March 3, 2008, http://www.jpost.com/Home/Article.aspx?id=96502; *Debbie Schlussel*, "Enough, Walid Shoebat: Why is Sean Hannity's Fake Terrorist Harassing Me?" September 16, 2008, http://www. debbieschlussel.com/4245/enough-walid-shoebat-why-is-sean-hannitys-fake-terrorist-harassing-me/.

84. Jerry Markon, "Justice Dept. Backs Muslim Teacher," *Washington Post*, March 23, 2011, 4.

85. Spencer Ackerman, "FBI Teaches Agents: 'Mainstream' Muslims Are

'Violent, Radical,'" *Wired*, September 14, 2011 http://www.wired.com/dangerroom/2011/09/fbi-muslims-radical/.

86. Spencer Ackerman, "Justice Department Official: Muslim 'Juries' Threaten 'Our Values,'" *Wired*, October 5, 2011, http://www.wired.com/dangerroom/2011/10/islamophobia-beyond-fbi/.

87. Dina Temple-Raston, "Terrorism Training Casts Pall over Muslim Employee," NPR, July 18, 2011, http://www.npr.org/2011/07/18/137712352/terrorism-training-casts-pall-over-muslim-employee.

88. Philips continued in his blog post to clarify his views: "With Islam, you have a religion that says kill the Jews, kill the infidels. It bothers me when a religion says kill the infidels." Justin Elliott, "Tea Party Nation Founder: I Have a Real Problem with Islam," *Slate*, October 27, 2010, http://www.salon.com/news/politics/war_room/2010/10/27/judson_phillilps_on_islam.

89. "How Dearborn, MI came to be under Sharia Law!," *Daily Kos*, October 12, 2010, http://www.dailykos.com/story/2010/10/12/232143/44.

90. Stephan Salisbury, "How Muslim-Bashing Loses Elections," *TomDispatch*, July 7, 2011, http://www.tomdispatch.com/archive/175418/.

91. Author interview with Juan Cole, January 28, 2011 (by phone), http://www.fpif.org/articles/interview_with_juan_cole.

92. Lee Fang, "Rep. King Says Muslims Aren't 'American' When It Comes to War," *ThinkProgress*, January 11, 2011, http://thinkprogress.org/politics/2011/01/11/138305/king-muslims-american/.

93. Michael McAuliff, "Peter King: I'm Not on a Witch Hunt," *New York Daily News*, March 6, 2011, http://www.nydailynews.com/blogs/dc/2011/03/pete-king-im-not-on-a-witch-hunt.

94. John Esposito, "Peter King's Hearings," *Washington Post*, March 6, 2011, http://onfaith.washingtonpost.com/onfaith/panelists/john_esposito/2011/03/islamophobia_draped_in_the_american_flag.html.

95. Jeff Spross et al., "The King's (Islamophobic) Speech, *Progress Report*, March 4, 2011, http://www.americanprogress.org/pr/2011/03/pr20110304.

96. MacKenzie Weinger, "In U.K., Peter King Defends Muslim Hearings," *Politico*, September 13, 2011, http://www.politico.com/news/stories/0911/63360.html.

97. For her latest venture, Geller is pushing a boycott of Campbell's Soup because it accepts *halal* certification—the Islamic version of kosher certification by a rabbi—from the Islamic Society of North America, a group which has gone out of its way to denounce religious extremism. Jayme Poisson, "Toronto-made Campbell's Soups Has U.S.

Conservatives Simmering," *Toronto Star*, October 19, 2010, http://www.thestar.com/news/article/877942--toronto-made-campbell-s-soups-has-u-s-conservatives-simmering.

98. Mitchell Bard, *The Arab Lobby*, x.

Chapter Five

1. This portrait of Andrew Berwick comes from several sources including: Lucy Carne, "Mass Killer Anders Behring Breivik Was 'Mummy's Boy' with Few Friends No Girlfriends before Norway Shooting," *Daily Telegraph*, July 26, 2011. http://www.dailytelegraph.com.au/news/mass-killer-anders-behring-breivik-was-mummys-boy-with-few-friends-no-girlfriends-before-norway-shooting/story-e6freuy9-1226101576263; Nick Carbone, "Bullying and Plastic Surgery: Childhood Friend Speaks Out on Anders Behring Breivik's Life," *Time*, July 26, 2011, http://newsfeed.time.com/2011/07/26/bullying-and-plastic-surgery-childhood-friend-speaks-out-on-anders-breiviks-life/ and "Anders Behring Breivik," Wikipedia, http://en.wikipedia.org/wiki/Anders_Behring_Breivik.

2. The manifesto, entitled "2083: A European Declaration of Independence," was distributed online in 2011; http://www.washingtonpost.com/r/2010-2019/WashingtonPost/2011/07/24/National-Politics/Graphics/2083+-+A+European+Declaration+of+Independence.pdf.

3. Fairness and Accuracy in Reporting, "Seeing 'Islamic Terror' in Norway," FAIR July 25, 2011, "http://www.fair.org/index.php?page=4359.

4. Jennifer Rubin, "Norway Bombing," *Washington Post*, July 22, 2011, http://www.washingtonpost.com/blogs/right-turn/post/norway-bombing/2011/03/29/gIQAB4D3TI_blog.html.

5. Jennifer Rubin, "Evil in Norway," *Washington Post*, July 23, 2011, http://www.washingtonpost.com/blogs/right-turn/post/evil-in-norway/2011/03/29/gIQAtsydVI_blog.html.

6. John Price and Michael Sandelson, "Former Progress Party Chairman in Muslim Quarrel," *Foreigner*, August 15, 2011, http://theforeigner.no/pages/news/former-progress-party-chairman-in-muslim-quarrel/.

7. Aslak Sira Myhre, "Time for Norway to Face Its Islamophobia," *Washington Post*, July 28, 2011, http://www.washingtonpost.com/opinions/time-for-norway-to-face-its-islamophobia/2011/07/27/gIQATFrsfI_story.html.

8. Oriana Fallaci, *The Rage and the Pride* (New York: Rizzoli, 2002), 148, 186.

9. George Gurley, "The Rage of Oriana Fallaci," *New York Observer*, January 26, 2003, http://www.observer.com/node/47020.

10. Bruce Bawer, "Inside the Mind of the Oslo Murderer," *Wall Street Journal*, July 25, 2011, http://online.wsj.com/article/SB10001424053111 903999904576465801154130960.html.

11. And many reviewers perceived it as such. "'The Rage and the Pride' is a bracing response to the moral equivocation, the multi-culti political correctness, the minimization and denial of the danger of Islamo-fascism that dogs the response to Sept. 11 and to the ongoing war on terrorism." Charles Taylor, "Oriana Fallaci Declares War on Radical Islam," *Salon*, November 16, 2002, http://dir.salon.com/books/feature/2002/11/16/ fallaci/.

12. David Levering Lewis, *God's Crucible*, 172.

13. Tomaz Mastnak, *Crusading Peace* (Berkeley: University of California Press, 2002), 227.

14. This slow-motion integration project did not, of course, include the half of Europe that the Soviet Union hauled into its sphere of influence, the "kidnapped West" in Milan Kundera's resonant phrase. Milan Kundera, "The Tragedy of Central Europe," *New York Review of Books*, April 26, 1984.

15. Ian Buruma, *Taming the Gods* (Princeton: Princeton University Press, 2010), 1–2.

16. Both projects had their illusory qualities. Europe established European citizenship with the Treaty of Maastricht in 1991, prepared for a monetary union with its own Europe-wide currency, and began accession discussions that would ultimately expand the EU by ten countries in 2004. But public discontent with European bureaucracy, opaque defense policies, and loss of national sovereignty threw sand into the gears of integration. The Euroskepticism born in the national referendums on the Maastricht Treaty in Denmark and France in 1992 became more powerful still in Ireland's initial rejection by referendum of the Lisbon Treaty in 1998. Although both treaties ultimately passed, Euroskepticism continues to serve as a brake on both deepening and widening integration. The United States, meanwhile, discovered that it could no longer dictate global economic policy in a world in which an integrated Europe and a rising China were becoming more dominant players.

17. Author interview with Massoud Shadjareh, December 4, 2010 (London), http://www.fpif.org/articles/ interview_with_the_islamic_human_rights_commission.

18. Jean-Marie Colombani, "We Are All Americans," *Le Monde*, September 12, 2001, http://www.worldpress.org/1101we_are_all_americans.htm.

19. "Millions Join Global Anti-War Protests," BBC, February 17, 2003, http://news.bbc.co.uk/2/hi/europe/2765215.stm; crowd estimates from

"February 15, 2003 anti-war protest," Wikipedia, http://en.wikipedia.
org/wiki/February_15,_2003_anti-war_protest.

20. Quoted in John Esposito, *The Future of Islam* (Oxford University Press,
2010), 26.

21. Orhan Pamuk, "The Souring of Turkey's European Dream," *Guardian*,
December 23, 2010, http://www.guardian.co.uk/commentisfree/2010/
dec/23/turkey-european-dream-migrants-minorites.

22. Christopher Caldwell, *Reflections on the Revolution in Europe*, 222.

23. Bat Ye'or, *Eurabia* (Cranbury, NJ: Associated University Presses, 2005), 9.

24. Kenichi Ohmae, *The End of the Nation State* (New York: Free Press,
1996); Jean-Marie Guéhenno, *The End of the Nation State* (Minneapolis:
University of Minnesota Press, 1995).

25. E. J. Hobsbawm, *Nations and Nationalism Since 1780* (Cambridge:
Cambridge University Press, 1990), 163.

26. See, for example, Richard Caplan and John Feffer, eds. *Europe's New
Nationalism* (New York: Oxford University Press, 1996).

27. Andrew Geddes, *The Politics of Migration and Immigration in Europe*
(London: Sage Publications, 2005), 17.

28. "Migration and Migrant Population Statistics," Eurostat, European
Commission, October 2010. http://epp.eurostat.ec.europa.eu/statistics_
explained/index.php/Migration_and_migrant_population_statistics.

29. Nearly half of the 31.9 million foreign-born people living in the
EU in 2009 came from countries ranking high in the UN's Human
Development Index (many of these coming from Russia, Albania, and
Turkey). Katya Vasileva, "Foreigners Living in the EU are Diverse and
Largely Younger than the Nationals of EU Member States," Eurostat,
European Commission, 2010. http://epp.eurostat.ec.europa.eu/cache/
ITY_OFFPUB/KS-SF-10-045/EN/KS-SF-10-045-EN.PDF.

30. Tariq Ramadan, *What I Believe* (New York: Oxford University Press, 2010), 13.

31. "Enoch Powell's 'Rivers of Blood' speech," *Independent*, November 6,
2007, http://www.telegraph.co.uk/comment/3643823/Enoch-Powells-
Rivers-of-Blood-speech.html.

32. Andrew Geddes, *The Politics of Migration and Immigration in Europe*, 60.

33. Pew Forum on Religion and Public Life, "Mapping the Global Muslim
Population," October 7, 2009, http://pewforum.org/PublicationPage.
aspx?id=1497.

34. John Esterbrook, " A Million French March Against Le Pen," CBS
News, May 1, 2002, http://www.cbsnews.com/stories/2002/04/23/world/
main506946.shtml; "Chirac landslide against Le Pen," CNN, May 6,
2002, http://edition.cnn.com/2002/WORLD/europe/05/05/france.win/
index.html.

35. Liz Fekete, *A Suitable Enemy* (London: Pluto: 2009), 59–60.

36. Ibid. 57–8.

37. Author interview with Arzu Merali, December 4, 2010, (London). http://www.fpif.org/articles/interview_with_the_islamic_human_rights_commission.

38. Christopher Caldwell, *Reflections on the Revolution in Europe*, 20.

39. "Sverigedemokraternas Officiella Reklamfilm, TV4," YouTube, September 12, 2010, http://www.youtube.com/user/sdwebbtv#p/u/15/hAhIZNofrKY.

40. "Sapone Antimmigrati," *Arezzo Notizie*, March 19, 2010, http://www.arezzonotizie.it/index.php?option=com_content&view=article&id=502 26:sapone-antimmigrati--nicotra-federazione-della-sinistra---monica-faenzi-condanni-iniziativa-lega-nord&catid=82:politica&Itemid=1085.

41. Pankaj Mishra, "Islamismism," *New Yorker*, June 7, 2010.

42. Quoted in Michael Slackman, "With Words on Muslims, Opening a Door Long Shut," *New York Times*, November 13, 2010.

43. Christopher Caldwell, *Reflections on the Revolution in Europe*, 168.

44. Anthony Faiola, "Anti-Muslim Feelings Propel Right Wing," *Washington Post*, October 26, 2010.

45. Benjamin Cunningham, "Islamophobia Surfaces Closer to Home," *Prague Post*, July 27, 2011, http://www.islamophobia-watch.com/islamophobia-watch/2011/7/28/right-wing-warns-against-threat-of-islamisation-in-the-czech.html; Czech News Agency, "Former Czech PM Sued over Statements on Islam," July 18, 2011, http://praguemonitor.com/2011/07/08/former-czech-pm-sued-over-statements-islam.

46. Bob Pitt, "Warsaw Mosque Protest: Buddhists Join Hands with Skinheads against Muslims," *Islamophobia Watch*, April 7, 2010, http://www.islamophobia-watch.com/islamophobia-watch/2010/4/7/warsaw-mosque-protest-buddhists-join-hands-with-skinheads-ag.html.

47. Boryana Dzhambazova, "Religious Minorities Suffer Violent Attacks from Bulgarian Nationalists," *Global Post*, June 11, 2011, http://www.globalpost.com/dispatch/news/regions/europe/110609/bulgaria-muslims-nationalists.

48. Benjamin Bruce, "Switzerland's Minaret Ban," Euro-Islam.info, http://www.euro-islam.info/key-issues/switzerlands-minaret-ban/.

49. Jeanne Kay, "Europe's Islamophobia," *Foreign Policy in Focus*, April 9, 2010, http://www.fpif.org/articles/europes_islamophobia.

50. "French Cabinet Backs Ban on Full Face Coverings," BBC, May 19, 2010, http://www.bbc.co.uk/news/10129324.

51. Tariq Ramadan, *What I Believe*, 98.

52. Estimates are for 2010; "Country Comparison: Total Fertility Rate," *CIA*

Fact Book, https://www.cia.gov/library/publications/the-world-factbook/rankorder/2127rank.html.

53. Pew estimated a rise from 6 to 8 percent. See Pew Forum on Religion & Public Life, "The Future of the Global Muslim Population," Pew Research Center, January 27, 2011, http://pewresearch.org/pubs/1872/muslim-population-projections-worldwide-fast-growth.

54. As characterized by Malise Ruthven, "The Big Muslim Problem!" *New York Review of Books*, December 17, 2009, 64.

55. "Ramadan—who plainly seeks to do for European Muslims what Jerry Falwell did for American evangelicals—argues strenuously for their increased involvement in European politics." See Bruce Bawer, *While Europe Slept* (NY: Broadway Books, 2006), 68.

56. Geert Wilders, "Enough is Enough: Ban the Koran," *Volkskrant*, August 8, 2007, http://www.militantislammonitor.org/article/id/3094.

57. Paul Hockenos, "Europe's Rising Islamophobia," *Nation*, May 9, 2011, 22–23.

58. Pew Global Attitudes Project, "Unfavorable Views of Jews and Muslims on the Increase in Europe," Pew Research Center September 17, 2008, http://pewglobal.org/2008/09/17/unfavorable-views-of-jews-and-muslims-on-the-increase-in-europe/.

59. Arthur Schlesinger, *The Disuniting of America* (New York: Norton, 1998).

60. "Cultural relativist scholars," argues Bassam Tibi, "fail to see that the new religious absolutism of Islam represents a new political religion that heralds a totalitarian threat to the open society." Bassam Tibi, "The Totalitarianism of Jihadist Islamism and Its Challenge to Europe and to Islam," in *Totalitarian Movements and Political Religions*, 8, no. 1 (2007), 41.

61. Samuel Huntington, *Who Are We?* (New York: Simon and Schuster, 2004), 171.

62. Ayaan Hirsi Ali, *Nomad* (New York: Free Press, 2010), xix.

63. *Shariah: The Threat to America*, 125; Dinesh D'Souza, *The Enemy at Home: The Cultural Left and Its Responsibility for 9/11* (New York: Doubleday, 2007), 2.

64. Steven Vertovec and Susanne Wessendorf , eds., *The Multicultural Backlash* (London: Routledge, 2010), 76–78.

65. Author interview with Arun Kundnani, January 13, 2010 (Washington, DC), http://www.fpif.org/articles/interview_with_arun_kundnani.

66. "It's easy to forget that in 1956 nineteen of twenty-two Southern senators signed a manifest odemandin the reversal of the decision, or that *The Atlantic Monthly*—a tribune of New England liberalism—published an article the same year arguing that Brown would promote interracial sex."

Jonathan Zimmerman, "What are Schools For?" *New York Review of Books*, October 14, 2010, 28.

67. John Burns, "Cameron Criticizes British 'Multiculturalism," *New York Times*, February 5, 2011, http://www.nytimes.com/2011/02/06/world/europe/06britain.html.

68. Peter Mandaville, "Muslim Youth in Europe" in Shireen Hunter, ed. Islam, *Europe's Second Religion* (Wesport, CT: Praeger, 2002), 22.

69. Jochen-Martin Gutsch, "The German Geert Wilders," *Der Spiegel Online*, January 6, 2011, http://www.spiegel.de/international/germany/0,1518,737676,00.html.

70. Dominic Casciani, "Who Are the English Defense League," BBC News, September 11, 2009, http://news.bbc.co.uk/2/hi/uk_news/magazine/8250017.stm; Mark Townsend, "English Defence League Forges Links with America's Tea Party," *Observer*, October 10, 2010, http://www.guardian.co.uk/uk/2010/oct/10/english-defence-league-tea-party.

71. Tony Blankley, *The West's Last Chance* (Washington, DC: Regnery, 2005), 24. Also Norman Podhoretz: "Conceivably the prospect of being conquered from within by Islamofascism will so concentrate the minds of the major West European countries that they will eventually join us in the fight against the threat from without." Norman Podhoretz, *World War IV*, 216.

72. See, for example, Christopher Deliso, *The Coming Balkan Caliphate* (Westport, CT: Praeger Security International, 2007) and Shaul Shay, *Islamic Terror and the Balkans* (New Brunswick, NJ: Transaction Books, 2007).

73. Daniel Pipes, *Militant Islam Reaches America*, 33.

74. Vali Nasr, *Forces of Fortune* (New York: Free Press, 2009), 110.

75. Author interview with Sule Kut, October 26, 2009 (Istanbul), http://balkansproject.ips-dc.org/?p=991.

76. Robert Dreyfuss, "U.S. Slams Turkey Over Iran," *Nation*, May 28, 2010, http://www.thenation.com/blog/us-slams-turkey-brazil-over-iran.

77. Helene Cooper, "U.S. Is Quietly Getting Ready for Syria without Assad," *New York Times*, September 20, 2011, http://www.nytimes.com/2011/09/20/world/middleeast/us-is-quietly-getting-ready-for-a-syria-without-an-assad.html?_r=2.

78. Stephen Zunes, "Democratic Party Defends Israeli Attack," *Foreign Policy in Focus*, June 10, 2010, http://www.fpif.org/articles/democratic_party_defends_israeli_attack.

79. "Report: Obama Gave Erdogan Ultimatum," *Jerusalem Post*, August 16, 2010, http://www.jpost.com/International/Article.aspx?id=184891.

80. At the time, he was lying on his back, semi-conscious, suffering from four

other bullet wounds. Account drawn from "Report of the international fact-finding mission to investigate violations of international law, including international humanitarian and human rights law, resulting from the Israeli attacks on the flotilla of ships carrying humanitarian assistance," Human Rights Council, UN General Assembly, September 27, 2010, http://www2.ohchr.org/english/bodies/hrcouncil/docs/15session/A.HRC.15.21_en.pdf.

81. "Turkish Economy and Investment Environment," Goldman Sachs, October 2008, http://www.taik.org/Default.aspx?mID=3&mSID=98&pgID=50&langid=1.

82. Paul Levin, *Turkey and the European Union*, 167–68.

83. European attitudes toward Turkey have warmed only slightly since 2009. According to the German-Marshall Fund 2011 Survey, the percentage of Europeans who saw Turkish accession as good reached 26 percent, compared to only 22 percent in 2005. See German-Marshall Fund, *Transatlantic Trends, Key Findings 2011*, 38; http://www.gmfus.org/publications_/TT/TT2011_final_web.pdf; German-Marshall Fund, *Transatlantic Trends, Key Findings 2005*, 9; http://trends.gmfus.org/doc/2005_english_key.pdf.

84. "Europe's Far-Right Vows to Push Referendum on Turkey's EU Accession," *Deutsche Welle*, October 23, 2010, http://www.dw-world.de/dw/article/0,,6142752,00.html.

85. Chris Patten, "No Way to Treat a Friend," *Guardian*, October 17, 2007, http://www.guardian.co.uk/commentisfree/2007/oct/17/comment.eu.

86. Bret Stephens, "What Is Happening to Turkey?" *Wall Street Journal*, May 1, 2010, http://pewforum.org/Religion-News/What-is-happening-to-Turkey-.aspx.

87. Thomas Friedman, "Letter from Istanbul," *New York Times*, June 15, 2010, http://www.nytimes.com/2010/06/16/opinion/16friedman.html; neocon pundit Liz Cheney even went so far as to create a new version of George W. Bush's "axis of evil" with Turkey, Iran, and Syria as the dark trinity. Greg Sargent, "Liz Cheney Attacks Obama for Saying Flotilla Deaths Were "Tragic," *Washington Post*, June 4, 2010, http://voices.washingtonpost.com/plum-line/2010/06/liz_cheney_attacks_obama_for_s.html.

88. As Stephen Kinzer writes, "The emerging conflict in Turkey is not over religion, but styles of power." See "Triumphant Turkey?" *New York Review of Books*, August 18, 2011, 37.

89. Omer Taspinar, "Turkish Gaullism?" *Today's Zaman*, April 12, 2011, http://www.brookings.edu/opinions/2010/0412_turkey_taspinar.aspx.

90. Sahin Alpay, "Is EU Accession the Main Goal of Turkish Foreign Policy?" *Sunday's Zaman*, November 15, 2010, http://www.todayszaman.com/columnist-227250-is-eu-accession-the-main-goal-of-turkish-foreign-policy.html; for the 2011 figure, see German-Marshall Fund, *Transatlantic Trends, Key Findings 2011*, 38.

91. Quoted in Kemal Kirisci, *Turkey's Foreign Policy in Turbulent Times, Institute for Security Studies*, 2006, http://www.iss.europa.eu/uploads/media/cp092.pdf.

Ending Crusade 2.0

1. Quoted in Karen Armstrong, *Holy War*, 187.
2. John Esposito, *The Islamic Threat*, 41.
3. Juan Cole, *Engaging the Muslim World*, 5.
4. Arthur Cohen, *The Myth of the Judeo-Christian Tradition* (New York: Schocken Books, 1971), xviii.
5. Ibid., xv–xvi.
6. Richard Cooper, "General Casts War in Religious Terms," *Los Angeles Times*, October 16, 2003. http://articles.latimes.com/2003/oct/16/nation/na-general16.
7. Jurgen Habermas, "Leadership and Leitkultur," *New York Times*, October 28, 2010, http://www.nytimes.com/2010/10/29/opinion/29Habermas.html?pagewanted=all.
8. Richard Bulliet, *The Case for Islamo-Christian Civilization* (New York: Columbia University Press, 2004), 15.
9. Norman Housley, *Contesting the Crusades* (Malden, MA: Blackwell, 2006), 157.
10. Tomaz Mastnak, *Crusading Peace* (Berkeley: University of California Press, 2002), 1–18. Indeed, Mastnak argues intriguingly that peacemaking and warmaking were in some sense two sides of the same coin, as the Council of Clermont in 1095 made exporting war to the Holy Land an essential part of maintaining peace and stability at home.
11. For more on the "trialogue" among the Abrahamic faiths see, e.g., Ismail Raji al Faruqi, *Trialogue of the Abrahamic Faiths* (Alexandria, VA: Al Sadawi Publications, 1991).
12. Robert Spencer, "Introduction" in Michael Radu, *Europe's Ghost* (New York: Encounter, 2009), v.
13. Edward Gibbon, *The Decline and Fall of the Roman Empire, Volume 6* (London: J. F. Dove, 1821), 470.
14. Martin Amis, *The Second Plane*, 9.
15. Richard Cohen, "A Democratic Egypt or a State of Hate," *Washington Post*, February 1, 2011, http://www.washingtonpost.com/wp-dyn/

content/article/2011/01/31/AR2011013104014.html.

16. Peter Beinart, *The Icarus Syndrome* (New York: Harper Collins, 2010), 9.

17. Joseph Stieglitz and Linda Bilmes, *The Three Trillion Dollar War* (New York: Norton, 2008); Christopher Hellman, "$1.2 Trillion Dollars for National Security," *TomDispatch*, March 1, 2011, http://www. tomdispatch.com/archive/175361/; Walter Pincus, "United States Needs to Reevaluate Assistance to Israel," *Washington Post*, October 17, 2011, http://www.washingtonpost.com/world/national-security/united-states-needs-to-reevaluate-its-assistance-to-israel/2011/10/15/gIQAK5XksL_ story.html.

18. Stephen Castle, "Cameron Backs Turkey Bid to Join EU," *New York Times*, July 27, 2010, http://www.nytimes.com/2010/07/28/world/ europe/28iht-britain.html?_r=1.

19. Paul Krugman, "Eurotrashed," *New York Times Magazine*, January 16, 2011.

20. Carl Bildt, Franco Frattini, William Hague, and Alexander Stubb, "Europe, Look Outward Again," *New York Times*, December 10, 2010, http://www.nytimes.com/2010/12/11/opinion/11iht-edbildt11.html.

21. Asli Bali, "Unpacking the Turkey's 'Court-Packing' Referendum," *Middle East Report*, November 5, 2010, http://www.merip.org/mero/ mero110510.html.

22. Quoted in European Stability Initiative newsletter, October 21, 2010, http://www.esiweb.org/index.php?lang=en&id=67&newsletter_ID=48.

23. Fareed Zakaria, "Fareed Zakaria's Letter to the ADL," *Newsweek*, August 6, 2010, http://www.newsweek.com/2010/08/06/fareed-zakaria-s-letter-to-the-adl.html.

24. "Katie Couric Speaks against Anti-Muslim Bigotry, Suggests Muslim 'Cosby Show,'" *Huffington Post*, January 1, 2011, http://www. huffingtonpost.com/2011/01/01/katie-couric-muslim-bigotry-cosby-show_n_803208.html.

25. John Esposito, *The Islamic Threat*, 43.

26. Alistair Crooke, *Resistance* (London: Pluto, 2009), 269.

Acknowledgments

Many people have helped this project along. The visionary Tom Engelhardt inspired me to pursue my initial research into Islamophobia and published my first essays at his inestimable TomDispatch website.

A number of readers generously devoted their time to critiquing drafts of the manuscript: Phyllis Bennis, Mughees Butt, Giuliana Chamedes, and Arun Kundnani. A succession of brilliant interns—Rebecca Adzham, Fatima Al-zeheri, Samer Araabi, Derek Bolton, Peter Certo, Noor Iqbal, Dominika Kruszewska, Derek Lyndes—helped with gathering materials, tracking down sources, and reading through reports. My colleagues at Foreign Policy in Focus and the Institute for Policy Studies provided feedback and support for my writing and research.

My editor at City Lights Greg Ruggiero has brilliantly guided this project from idea to implementation, and a big thanks to the rest of the City Lights team for getting this book into the world.

My deepest debt of gratitude is to Karin Lee who not only read these pages but challenged me at every point to make this book clearer, more convincing, and more useful. She has contributed more than anyone to the care and feeding of this project.

If this book suffers from any inadequacies, they are due to my ignoring the advice of everyone listed above.

Bibliography

Abbas, Tahir, ed. *Muslim Britain*. London: Zed, 2006.

Abdo, Geneive. *Mecca and Main Street: Muslim Life in America after 9/11*. Oxford: Oxford University Press, 2007.

Ackerman, Spencer. "FBI Teaches Agents: 'Mainstream' Muslims Are 'Violent, Radical.'" *Wired*, September 14, 2011.

Ackerman, Spencer. "Unprecedented' Drone Assault." *Wired*, December 17, 22010.

Ahmed, Akbar S. "Bridgebuilder to the Muslim World." *beliefnet*, 2005.

Ahmed, Akbar S. *Journey into America*. Washington, DC: Brookings Institution, 2010.

Akbarzadeh, Shahram, and Fethi Mansouri. *Islam and Political Violence: Muslim Diaspora and Radicalism in the West*. London: Tauris Academic Studies, 2007.

Alpay, Sahin. "Is EU Accession the Main Goal of Turkish Foreign Policy?" *Sunday's Zaman*, November 15, 2010.

Ali, Ayaan Hirsi. *Nomad*. New York: Free Press, 2010.

Ali, Tariq. *The Clash of Fundamentalisms*. New York: Verso, 2002.

Ali, Wajahat, Eli Clifton, Matthew Duss, Lee Fang , Scott Keyes, and Faiz Shakir, *Fear, Inc.* Washington DC: Center for American Progress, 2011.

Alston, Philip. "Report of the Special Rapporteur on Extrajudicial, Summary or Arbitrary Executions." UN General Assembly, Human Rights Council, 2010.

Altman, Alex. "TIME Poll: Majority Oppose Mosque, Many Distrust Muslims." *Time*, 2010.

Amis, Martin. *The Second Plane*. New York: Knopf, 2008.

Armstrong, Karen. *Holy War*. New York: Doubleday, 1992.

Armstrong, Karen. "We Cannot Afford to Maintain These Ancient Prejudices against Islam." *Guardian*, September 17, 2006.

Aslan, Reza. *No God but God*. New York: Random House, 2005.

Bali, Asli. "Unpacking the Turkey's 'Court-Packing' Referendum." *Middle East Report*, November 5, 2010.

Bakalian, Anny P., and Mehdi Bozorgmehr. *Backlash 9/11: Middle Eastern and Muslim Americans Respond*. Berkeley: University of California, 2009.

Baraz, Daniel. *Medieval Cruelty*. Ithaca, NY: Cornell University Press, 2003.

Bard, Mitchell. *The Arab Lobby*. New York: Harper, 2010.

Bawer, Bruce. "Inside the Mind of the Oslo Murderer." *Wall Street Journal*, June 25, 2011.

Bawer, Bruce. *While Europe Slept*. New York: Broadway Books, 2006.

Beinart, Peter. *The Good Fight*. New York: Harper Collins, 2006.

Beinart, Peter. *The Icarus Syndrome*. New York: Harper Collins, 2010.

Belden, David. "Backward Christian Soldiers." *Humanist*, January/February, 2008.

Berman, Paul, *Flight of the Intellectuals*. Melville House, 2010.

Berman, Paul. *Terror and Liberalism*. New York: Norton, 2003.

Bildt, Carl et al. "Europe, Look Outward Again." *New York Times*, December 10, 2010.

Blankley, Tony. *The West's Last Chance*. Washington, DC: Regnery, 2005.

Blanks, David and Michael Frassetto, eds. *Western Views of Islam in Medieval and Early Modern Europe*. New York: St. Martin's Press, 1999.

Blumenthal, Max. "The Great Fear." *TomDispatch*, December 19, 2010.

Bohn, Michael. *The Achille Lauro Hijacking. Dulles*, VA: Brassey's, 2004.

Bonney, Richard. *False Prophets: The 'Clash of Civilizations' and the Global War on Terror*. Oxford, Peter Lang, 2008.

Brayton, Ed. "Controversial Experts Authored 'Shariah' Report Hailed by Bachmann." *Minnesota Independent*, 2010.

Breivik, Anders Behring. "2083: A European Declaration of Independence." A. Breivik, 2011.

Brock, David. *Blinded by the Right*. New York: Crown, 2002.

Brown, Janelle. "Anti-Arab Passions Sweep the US." *Salon*, September 13, 2001.

Bruce, Benjamin. "Switzerland's Minaret Ban." *Euro-Islam.info*, 2009.

Bruckner, Pascal, *The Tyranny of Guilt*. Princeton, NJ: Princeton University Press, 2010

Bulliet, Richard. *The Case for Islamo-Christian Civilization*. New York: Columbia University Press, 2004.

Bunzl, Matti, *Anti-Semitism and Islamophobia*. Chicago: Prickly Paradigm Press, 2007.

Buruma, Ian. *Taming the Gods*. Princeton, NJ: Princeton University Press,

2010.

Cainkar, Louise. *Homeland Insecurity: The Arab American and Muslim American Experience after 9/11*. New York: Russell Sage Foundation, 2009.

CAIR's Anti-Terrorism Campaigns, http://www.cair.com/AmericanMuslims/AntiTerrorism.aspx.

Caldwell, Christopher, *Reflections on the Revolution in Europe*. New York: Doubleday, 2009.

Caplan, Richard and John Feffer, *Europe's New Nationalism*. New York: Oxford University Press, 1996.

Cesari, Jocelyne. *When Islam and Democracy Meet: Muslims in Europe and in the United States*. New York: Palgrave Macmillan, 2004. Print.

Cline, Edward. "The Fascists in our Midst." Center for the Advancement of Capitalism, August 15, 2006.

Cockburn, Alexander. "The Tenth Crusade." *Counterpunch*, September 7, 2002.

Cohen, Arthur. *The Myth of Judeo-Christian Tradition*. New York: Schocken Books, 1971.

Cole, David. "Are We Safer?" *New York Review of Books*, March 9, 2006.

Cole, Juan. *Engaging the Muslim World*. New York: Palgrave, 2009.

Colombani, Jean-Marie. "We Are All Americans." *Le Monde*, September 12, 2001.

"Combating Extremists." *OIC Journal*, September–December 2009.

Conetta, Carl. *Strange Victory*. Boston: Project on American Defense Alternatives, 2002.

Conover, Ted. "The Pathetic Newburgh Four." *Slate*, November 23, 2010.

Conte, Michaelangelo. "State Court Throws out Religion as Defense." *Jersey Journal*, August 2, 2010.

Cook, Blanche Wiesen. *The Declassified Eisenhower*. New York: Doubleday, 1981.

Coulter, Ann "This Is War" *National Review*, September 13, 2001.

Council on American Islamic Relations. "Same Hate, Different Target." 2010.

Crooke, Alistair. *Resistance*. London: Pluto, 2009.

Curry, Jerry. "Islam is a Violent Religion." *WebToday*, September 11, 2010.

Curtis, Edward. "Five Myths about Mosques in America." *Washington Post*, August 29, 2010.

Curtis, Edward. *Muslims in America*. New York: Oxford University Press,

2009.

Daniel, Norman. *Islam and the West*. Oxford: OneWorldPublications, 1993.

Darwish, Nonie. *Now They Call Me Infidel*. New York: Penguin, 2006.

De Young, Karen and Jaffe, Greg. "US Secret War Expands Globally as Special Operations Forces Take Larger Role." *Washington Post*, June 4, 2010.

Deliso, Christopher. *The Coming Balkan Caliphate*. Westport, CT: Praeger Security International, 2007.

Djerejian, Edward. *Danger and Opportunity*. New York: Simon and Schuster, 2008.

"Dossier of Civilian Casualties in Iraq 2003–2005." Iraq Body Count, 2005.

Dreyfuss, Robert. *Devil's Game*. New York: Metropolitan, 2005.

Dreyfuss, Robert. "US Slams Turkey Over Iran." *Nation*, May 28, 2010.

D'Souza, Dinesh. *The Enemy at Home: The Cultural Left and Its Responsibility for 9/11*. New York: Doubleday, 2007.

Elliot, Justin. "How the Ground Zero Mosque Fear Mongering Began." *Salon*, August 16, 2010.

Elliott, Justin. "Tea Party Nation Founder: I Have a Real Problem with Islam." *Slate*, October 27, 2010.

Emerson, Steven. *American Jihad*. New York: Free Press, 2002.

Erlich, Reese. "Conversations with Terrorists." PoliPoint Press, 2010.

Esposito, John. *The Future of Islam*. New York: Oxford University Press, 2010. Print.

Esposito, John, and Ibrahim Kalin, eds. *Islamophobia*. New York: Oxford University Press, 2011.

Esposito, John. *The Islamic Threat*. New York: Oxford University Press, 1999.

Esposito, John, and Dalia Mogahed. *Who Speaks for Islam?* New York: Gallup Press, 2007.

"Europe's Far-Right Vows to Push Referendum on Turkey's EU Accession." *Deutsche Welle*, October 23, 2010.

Fadl, Khaled Abou El et al. *The Place of Tolerance in Islam*. Boston: Beacon, 2002.

Faiola, Anthony. "Anti-Muslim Feelings Propel Right Wing." *Washington Post*, October 26, 2010.

Fallaci, Oriana. *The Rage and the Pride*. New York: Rizzoli, 2002.

Faludi, Susan. *The Terror Dream*. New York: MacMillan, 2007.

Faruqi, Ismail Raji. *Trialogue of the Abrahamic Faiths*. Alexandria, VA: Al Sadawi Publications, 1991.

Feffer, John. *Beyond Detente*. New York: Noon Day Press, 1990.

Fekete, Liz. *A Suitable Enemy: Racism, Migration and Islamophobia in Europe*. London: Pluto, 2009.

Feldman, Noah. *After Jihad*. New York: Farrar, Straus, Giroux, 1993.

Feldman, Noah. *The Fall and Rise of the Islamic State*. Princeton, NJ: Princeton University Press, 2008.

Friedman, Thomas. "Letter From Istanbul." *New York Times*, June 15, 2010.

Friedman, Thomas. *The World is Flat*. New York: Farrar, Straus, Giroux, 2007.

Frum, David. *The Right Man*. New York: Random House, 2005.

Fukuyama, Francis. *The End of History and the Last Man*. New York: Avon, 1992.

Fuller, Graham. *A World without Islam*. New York: Little, Brown, 2010.

"Fundamentalist Menace." *Times*, 1990.

Gabriel, Theodore, and Ron Geaves. *Islam and the West Post 9/11*. Aldershot: Ashgate, 2006.

Gaddis, John Lewis. *Strategies of Containment*. New York: Oxford University Press, 1982.

Gaffney, Frank. "America's First Muslim President?" *Washington Times*, June 9, 2009.

Gantz, Jeremy. "Terrorist by Association." *In These Times*, December 13, 2010.

Geddes, Andrew. *The Politics of Migration and Immigration in Europe*. London: Sage Publications, 2005.

Gerecht, Reuel Marc. *The Islamic Paradox*. Washington, DC: American Enterprise Institute Press, 2004.

Gerges, Fawaz. *The Rise and Fall of Al-Qaeda*. New York: Oxford University Press, 2011.

Ghosh, Bobby. "Is America Islamaphobic?" *Time*, August 30, 2010.

Gibbon, Edward. *The Decline and Fall of the Roman Empire, Volume 6*. London: J. F. Dove, 1821.

Gladwell, Malcolm. *Blink*. New York: Little, Brown, 2005.

Goldman Sachs. "Turkish Economy and Investment Environment." *taik. org*, 2008.

Goody, Jack. *Islam in Europe*. London: Polity, 2004.

Gottschalk, Peter, and Gabriel Greenberg. *Islamophobia: Making Muslims the Enemy*. Lanham: Rowman & Littlefield, 2008.

Griswold, Eliza. *The Tenth Parallel*. New York: Farrar, Straus, Giroux, 2010.

Gurley, George. "The Rage of Oriana Fallaci." *New York Observer*, January 26, 2003.

Gutsch, Jochen-Martin. "The German Geert Wilders." *Der Spiegel Online*, January 6, 2011.

Hagopian, Elaine Catherine. *Civil Rights in Peril: The Targeting of Arabs and Muslims*. Chicago: Haymarket, 2004.

Hamdon, Evelyn Leslie. *Islamophobia and the Question of Muslim Identity: the Politics of Difference and Solidarity*. Black Point, NS: Fernwood, 2010.

Hamid, Mohsin. *The Reluctant Fundamentalist*. Orlando: Houghton Mifflin Harcourt, 2008.

Herf, Jeffrey. *Nazi Propaganda for the Arab World*. New Haven, CT: Yale University Press, 2009.

Hervik, Peter. *The Annoying Difference*. New York: Berghahn Books, 2011.

Hobsbawm, E. J. *Nations and Nationalism since 1780*. Cambridge: Cambridge University Press, 1990.

Hockenos, Paul. "Europe's Rising Islamophobia." *Nation*. May 9, 2011.

Housley, Norman. *Contesting the Crusades*. Malden, MA: Blackwell, 2006.

Howard, Philip. *The Digital Origins of Dictatorships and Democracy*. New York: Oxford University Press, 2010.

Human Rights Watch. *We Are Not the Enemy*. Human Rights Watch, 2002.

Huntington, Samuel. *The Clash of Civilizations and the Remaking of World Order*. New York: Simon and Schuster, 1996.

Huntington, Samuel. *Who Are We?* New York: Simon and Schuster, 2004.

Ignatieff, Michael. *Empire Lite*. New York: Vintage, 2003.

"Islamic Calvinists." *European Stability Initiative*. September 19, 2005.

Jalal, Ayesha. *Partisans of Allah*. Cambridge: Harvard University Press, 2008.

Jamal, Amaney and Nadine Naber. *Race and Arab-Americans after 9/11*. Syracuse, NY: Syracuse University Press, 2008.

The Jerusalem Bible. New York: Doubleday, 1968.

Jewett, Thomas. "Terrorism in Early America." *Early America Review*, Winter/Spring 2002.

Kagan, Robert. *Dangerous Nation*. New York: Knopf, 2006.

Kaplan, Fred. "The Professional." *New York Times Magazine*, February 10, 2008.

"Katie Couric Speaks Against Anti-Muslim Bigotry, Suggests Muslim 'Cosby Show.'" *Huffington Post*, January 1, 2011.

Kay, Jeanne. "Europe's Islamaphobia." *Foreign Policy in Focus*, April 9, 2010.

Kennedy, Paul. *The Rise and Fall of Great Powers*. New York: Random House, 1987.

Kinzer, Stephen. *Crescent and Star*. New York: Farrar, Straus and Giroux, 2008.

Kinzer, Stephen. *Reset: Iran, Turkey, and America's Future*. New York: Times Books, 2010.

Kinzer, Stephen. "Triumphant Turkey?" *New York Review of Books*, 2011.

Kirisci, Kemal. Turkey's Foreign Policy in Turbulent Times, Institute for Security Studies, 2006.

Kirkpatrick, Jeanne. *Dictatorships and Double Standards*. New York: Simon and Schuster, 1982.

Kitzen, Michael. *Tripoli and the United States at War*. Jefferson, NC: McFarland, 1993.

Koppelman, Alex. "Why the Stories about Obama's Birth Certificate Will Never Die." *Salon*, December 5, 2008.

Krauthammer, Charles. "The Unipolar Moment." *Foreign Affairs*, 1991.

Kristof, Nicholas. "Message to Muslims: I'm Sorry." *New York Times*, September 18, 2010.

Kristol, William and Kagan, Robert. "Toward a Neo-Reaganite Foreign Policy." *Foreign Affairs*, 1996.

Krugman, Paul. "Eurotrashed." *New York Times Magazine*, January 16, 2011.

Kull, Steven. "Muslims and America: Internalizing the Clash of Civilizations." *World Public Opinion*, June 7, 2010.

Kundera, Milan. "The Tragedy of Central Europe." *New York Review of Books*, April 26, 1984.

Kundnani, Arun. "The FBI's 'Good' Muslims." *Nation*. September 19, 2011.

Kundnani, Arun. "Islamism and the Roots of Liberal Rage." *Race and Class*, October 2008.

Kurzman, Charles, David Schanzer, and Ebrahim Moosa. "Muslim

American Terrorism Since 9/11: Why So Rare?" *Muslim World*, 2011.

Lambert, Frank. *The Barbary Wars*. New York: Hill and Wang, 2005.

Leiken, Robert, and Brooke, Steven. "The Moderate Muslim Brotherhood." *Foreign Affairs*, March/April 2007.

Levesque-Alam, Junaid M. "Robert Wright and the Koran." *Foreign Policy in Focus*, September 15, 2010.

Levi-Strauss, Claude. *Tristes Tropiques*. New York: Washington Square Press, 1977.

Levin, Paul. *Turkey and the European Union*. New York: Palgrave MacMillan, 2011.

Lewis, David Levering. *God's Crucible*. New York: Norton, 2008.

Lewis, Bernard. *The Assassins*. New York: Basic, 2002.

Lewis, Bernard. "Communism and Islam." In Walter Laqueur, *The Middle East in Transition*, Freeport, NY: Books for Libraries Press, 1971.

Lewis, Bernard. *Faith and Power*. New York: Oxford University Press, 2010.

Lewis, Bernard. "The Roots of Muslim Rage." *Atlantic*, September 1990.

"Liddy Guest Walid Shoebat Falsely Claimed that Obama Is 'Definitely a Muslim.'" *Media Matters*, September 11, 2008.

"Limbaugh Calls Islamic Center a 'Victory Monument at Ground Zero.'" *Media Matters*, August 17, 2010.

Littwak, Robert. *Rogue States and US Foreign Policy*. Washington, DC: Woodrow Wilson Center Press, 2000.

London, Joshua. "America's Earliest Terrorists." *National Review*, December 16, 2005.

Maalouf, Amin. *The Crusades through Arab Eyes*. New York: Schocken Books, 1985.

Madhani, Aamer. "Is Obama's Outreach to Muslims Working?" *National Journal*, 2010.

Majid, Anouar. *We Are All Moors: Ending Centuries of Crusades Against Muslims and Other Minorities*. Minneapolis: University of Minnesota Press, 2009.

Malik, Iftikhar Haider. *Crescent between Cross and Star: Muslims and the West after 9/11*. Karachi: Oxford University Press, 2006.

Mamdani, Mahmood. *Good Muslim, Bad Muslim: America, the Cold War, and the Roots of Terror*. New York: Three Leaves, 2004.

Mandaville, Peter. "Muslim Youth in Europe." In *Islam, Europe's Second Religion*, edited by Shireen Hunter. Westport, CT: Praeger, 2002.

Manji, Irshad. *The Trouble with Islam*. New York: St. Martin's, 2003.

Mansfield, Peter. *The Arabs*. London: Penguin, 1985.

Martin, Richard, and Abbas Barzegar. *Islamism*. Stanford: Stanford University Press, 2010.

Mastnak, Tomaz. *Crusading Peace*. Berkeley: University of California Press, 2002.

"Migration and migrant population statistics." *Eurostat*, European Commission, October 2010.

Mishra, Pankaj. "Islamismism." *New Yorker*, June 7, 2010.

Munro, Dana C. *Urban and the Crusaders: Translations and Reprints from the Original Sources of European History*. Philadelphia: University of Pennsylvania, 1895.

Nasr, Seyyed Vali Reza. *Forces of Fortune: The Rise of the New Muslim Middle Class and What It Will Mean for Our World*. New York: Free, 2009.

Netherlands Scientific Council for Government Policy, Dynamism in Islamic Activism. Amsterdam: Amsterdam University Press, 2006.

Nimer, Mohamed. *Islamophobia and Anti-Americanism: Causes and Remedies*. Beltsville, MD.: Amana Publications, 2007.

Ohmae, Kenichi and Guehenno, Jean-Marie. *The End of the Nation State*. New York: Free Press, 1996.

Pal, Amitabh. *"Islam" Means Peace*. New York: Praeger, 2011.

Pamuk, Orhan. "The Souring of Turkey's European Dream." *Guardian*, December 23, 2010.

Pape, Robert. "What Triggers the Suicide Bomber?" *Los Angeles Times*, October 22, 2010.

Patten, Chris. "No Way to Treat a Friend." *Guardian*, October 17, 2007.

Pew Forum on Religion and Public Life. "Mapping the Global Muslim Population." Pew Global, 2009.

Pew Global Attitudes Project. "Obama More Popular Abroad Than At Home, Global Image of US Continues to Benefit." Pew Global, 2010.

Pfaff, William. "Manufacturing Insecurity." *Foreign Affairs*, November/December 2010.

Pipes, Daniel. "A Madrassah Grows in Brooklyn." *New York Sun*, April 24, 2007.

Pipes, Daniel. *Militant Islam Reaches America*. New York: Norton, 2002.

Pipes, Daniel. "The Muslims are Coming, the Muslims are Coming." *National Interest*, 1990.

Podhoretz, Norman. *World War IV.* New York: Doubleday, 2007.

Podliska, Bradley. *Acting Alone.* Lanham, MD: Lexington Books, 2010.

Polo, Marco et al. *The Travels of Marco Polo.* New York: Alfred A. Knopf, 2008.

Posner, Sarah. "Welcome to the Shari'ah Conspiracy Theory Industry." *Religious Dispatches.* March 18, 2011.

Powell, Enoch. "Rivers of Blood Speech." *Independent*, 2007.

Priest, Dana, and Arkin, William. "Monitoring America." *Washington Post*, December 20, 2010.

The Qur'an. New York: Penguin, 1981.

Qureshi, Emran, and Michael Anthony Sells. *The New Crusades: Constructing the Muslim Enemy.* New York: Columbia University Press, 2003.

Radu, Michael. *Europe's Ghost.* New York: Encounter Books, 2009.

Ramadan, Tariq. *What I Believe.* New York: Oxford University Press, 2010.

Rauf, Feisal Abudl. *What's Right with Islam.* San Francisco: Harper Collins, 2004.

"Richard Dawkins on Islam." *faithfreedom.org*, 2010.

Runciman, Steven. *The First Crusade.* New York: Cambridge University Press, 2005.

Runciman, Steven. *A History of the Crusades: Volume 3.* Cambridge: Cambridge University Press, 1951.

Runnymede Trust. *Islamophobia: A Challenge for Us All.* London: Runnymede Trust, 1997.

Ruthven, Malise, "The Birth of Islam: A Different View." *New York Review of Books.* April 7, 2011.

Ruthven, Malise. "The Big Muslim Problem!" *New York Review of Books*, December 17, 2009.

Ruthven, Malise. "Faith and Reason: Construing Islam as a Language." *Independent*, 1990.

Ruthven, Malise "Righteous and Wrong," *New York Review of Books*, August 19, 2010.

Sacirbey, Omar. "Skeptics Challenge Life Stories Offered by High-Profile Muslim Converts to Christianity." *Washington Post*, June 26, 2010.

Said, Edward. *Covering Islam: How the Media and the Experts Determine How We See the Rest of the World.* New York: Vintage, 1997.

Said, Edward. *Orientalism.* New York: Vintage, 1979.

Salisbury, Stephan. "How Muslim-Bashing Loses Elections." *TomDispatch*,

2011.

Salisbury, Stephan. *Mohamed's Ghosts*. New York: Nation Books, 2010.

Salisbury, Stephan. "Plotting Terrorism." *TomDispatch*, July 6, 2010.

Schanzer, David, Charles Kurzman and Ebrahim Moosa. *Anti-Terror Lessons of Muslim-Americans*, 2010.

Schlesinger, Arthur. *The Disuniting of America*. New York: Norton, 1998.

Scoliono, Elaine. "Seeing Green." *New York Times Magazine*, Jamuary 21, 1996.

Semmerling, Tim Jon. "*Evil*" *Arabs in American Popular Film: Orientalist Fear*. Austin: University of Texas, 2006.

Shaheen, Jack G. *Reel Bad Arabs: How Hollywood Vilifies a People*. New York: Olive Branch, 2001.

Shariah: The Threat to America. Center for Security Policy, 2010.

Shay, Shaul. *Islamic Terror and the Balkans*, New Brunswick, NJ: Transaction Books, 2007.

Shienbaum, Kim Ezra, and Jamal Hasan. *Beyond Jihad*. Bethesda, MD: Academica Press, 2006.

The Song of Roland. New York: Penguin, 1983.

Spencer, Robert. *The Politically Incorrect Guide to Islam*. Washington, DC: Regnery, 2005.

Spencer, Robert. *The Truth about Muhammad*. Washington, DC: Regnery, 2006.

Stephens, Bret. "What is Happening to Turkey?" *Wall Street Journal*, May 1, 2010.

Sultan, Wafa. *A God Who Hates*. New York: St. Martin's, 2003.

Taspinar, Omer. "Turkish Gaullism?" *Today's Zaman*, April 12, 2010.

Taylor, Charles. "Oriana Fallaci Declares War on Radical Islam." *Salon*, November 16, 2002.

Tehranian, John. *Whitewashed: America's Invisible Middle Eastern Minority*. New York: New York University Press, 2009.

Economist. "Islam and Democracy: Uneasy Companions," 2011, economist.com/.

Tibi, Bassam. "The Totalitarianism of Jihadist Islam and its Challenge to Europe and Islam." *Totalitarian Movements and Political Religions*, 8, no.1 (2007).

Tolan, John. *Saracens*. New York: Columbia University Press, 2002.

Toth, Anthony. "On Arabs and Islam." *Washington Report on Middle Eastern Affairs*, January 1987.

Townsend, Mark. "English Defence League Forges Links with America's Tea Party," *Observer*, October 10, 2010.

"Transcript of President Bush's Address," CNN, September 21, 2001.

Triandafyllidou, Anna, ed. *Muslims in 21st Century Europe*. New York: Routledge, 2010.

"2010: The Year of the Drone." New America Foundation, counterterriorismnewamerica.net/.

Tyerman, Christopher. *God's War*. Cambridge, MA: Harvard University Press, 2006.

Vertovec, Steven, and Susanne Wessendorf. *The Multicultural Backlash*. London: Routledge, 2010.

Vidino, Lorenzo. *The New Muslim Brotherhood in the West*. New York: Columbia University Press, 2010.

Vlahos, Kelley. "Tension between FBI and Muslims over Entrapment Charges Growing." *Change.org*, December 7, 2010.

Vogel, Kenneth, and Giovanni Russonello. "Latest Mosque Issue: The Money Trail," *Politico*, September 5, 2010.

Walt, Stephen. "Why They Hate Us II." *Foreign Policy*. 2009.

Welch, Michael. *Scapegoats of September 11th: Hate Crimes & State Crimes in the War on Terror*. New Brunswick, NJ: Rutgers University Press, 2006.

Wells, Colin. *Sailing to Byzantium*. New York: Random House, 2006.

Wilders, Geert. "Enough is Enough: Ban the Koran." *Volkskrant*, August 8, 2007.

World Islamic Front. "Jihad against Jews and Crusaders." *fas.org*, 1998.

Worth, Robert. "Preaching Moderate Islam and Becoming a TV Star." *New York Times*, January 2, 2009.

Ye'or, Bat. *Eurabia*. Madison: Fairleigh Dickinson University Press, 2005.

Zaharna, R. S. *Battles to Bridges*. New York: Palgrave MacMillan, 2010.

Zakaria, Fareed. "Fareed Zakaria's Letter to the ADL." *Newsweek*, 2010.

Zogby, James. "It's a Damn Shame." *Huffington Post*, August 6, 2010.

Zunes, Stephen. "Democratic Party Defends Israeli Attack." *Foreign Policy in Focus*, June 20, 2010.

Zurcher, Erik. *Turkey: A Modern History*. London: I. B. Tauris, 2005.

Index

"Passim" (literally "scattered") indicates intermittent discussion of a topic over a cluster of pages.

ABOUT THE AUTHOR

John Feffer is the codirector of Foreign Policy in Focus at the Institute for Policy Studies. He will be an Open Society fellow beginning in 2012.

He is the author of several books, including *North Korea, South Korea: U.S. Policy at a Time of Crisis* (Seven Stories, 2003) and numerous articles in the *New York Times*, *Boston Globe*, Salon, the *American Prospect*, the *Nation*, TomDispatch, the *Washington Post* and other publications. He has been a writing fellow at Provisions Library in Washington DC and a PanTech fellow in Korean Studies at Stanford University. He is a former associate editor of *World Policy Journal*. He has worked as an international affairs representative in Eastern Europe and East Asia for the American Friends Service Committee.

He has been interviewed widely on television and radio, including CNN, MSNBC, al-Jazeera, Democracy Now, and elsewhere. He is a recipient of the Herbert W. Scoville fellowship and has been a writer in residence at Blue Mountain Center and the Wurlitzer Foundation.